DEATHWALKER

Journeys of Life, Death & Beyond

Theresa Dominguez-Weiss

Deathwalker—Journeys of Life, Death & Beyond
Published by Power Places
Denver, Colorado

First Edition, August 2020
ISBN: 978-1-7351593-0-0
BODY, MIND & SPIRIT / General

Front cover design: Theresa Dominguez-Weiss
Back cover design: Theresa Dominguez-Weiss
Drawings: Inna Shirokova

POWER PLACES®

"What we call the beginning is often the end.
And to make an end is to make a beginning.
The end is where we start from."

T.S. ELIOT

To my beloved husband Toby who 41 years ago
re-ignited *"awareness"* of Power Places®
around the world.

"An adventure is only an
inconvenience rightly considered.
An inconvenience is only an adventure
wrongly considered."

"The world will never starve for want of
wonders; but only for want of wonder."

G.K. CHESTERTON

CONTENTS

Introduction

When my beloved Grandma Rosie died I had the most extraordinary experience. It was so overwhelming and so unheard of to me that I completely shut it out of my mind. Triggered by a professional experience almost 2 decades later, the memory of those moments right after my "Abuelita" (grandmother in Spanish) died started to bubble up to the surface

It was while I was in Crete the week of March 25, 1999 directing Power Places® international conference with the theme of "Life, Death & Beyond." Neale Donald Walsch, author of "Conversations with God'" was the keynote speaker. During the conference days wisps of memories of what had occurred the moment Grandma Rosie died started to seep through. Those memories made me very uncomfortable. I felt what had happened made me "strange and weird." Yet there was a deep longing to remember what occurred.

One afternoon I was having lunch with Neale and decided to say something. I figured if he was the person who had "Conversations with God," he'd be the one to speak to!

So we're sitting there eating and I start to tell him that I was having memories come up of a strange experience I had when my grandmother died. Something I'd repressed for years as it was just too weird. I think I said something to the effect that I took her to the OtherSide.

For a few minutes I struggled to put into logical sentences what I didn't understand myself. For the most part, Neale slowly kept eating his lunch, briefly glancing at me every moment or so. I quickly ran out of anything else to say. Neale put his fork down and said something to the effect if I wrote it he would look at it.

I abruptly left the table, went to my room, sat down taking some hotel stationery out. I still remember glancing at the blank sheet of paper as the pen hit its mark and the first sentence came pouring out, unbidden. My pen took on a life of it's own as most of the first chapter came out that afternoon, as is.

That led to writing remembrances of other personal "transformative" occurrences. Experiences that would be considered by most to be outside the realm of ordinary day to day life.

These episodes include a 5 year old beloved patient dying in front of me as a young nurse of 19, a fellow 7th grader committing suicide, experiences at ancient mystical sites such as the Great Pyramid, and the Temple of the Sun at Machu Picchu, and a chapter about telepathy and communications with two treasured pets. Then there's my eye-witness account to a "near death" experience of a group member outside 2,500 year old Edfu Temple on the Nile.

I admit many of these experiences sound really out there and could be misconstrued as the ramblings of a schizophrenic psychotic. However, people in my life, personally and professionally, consider me a psychologically balanced person and of sound mind.

These experiences are not "breaks" in my mind or rifts in my mental health. Rather I refer to these out-of-the-ordinary, or "peak" life moments as shamanic transformative experiences. Ultimately uplifting, these occurrences provided baby-steps and sometimes great spring-boards into what has resulted into a "meaningful life."

Throughout my life I have found myself in situations around death and dying. As a 16 year old volunteer candy-striper at the local hospital, working in convalescent homes to put myself through college, and then stints as an RN working in Intensive Care, Labor and Delivery, Emergency Room, acute Coronary Care, and rehabilitation units, I have seen death firsthand and I have witnessed births. Those who have had similar experiences will agree that these are profound moments. Something happens that is outside the ordinary realm of our day to day life.

For over 20 years I practiced nursing in Los Angeles area hospitals. In the early 80's I obtained an advanced certificate for Nurse Practitioner from University of California, Davis' Medical School in Family Practice, (FNP). My first job as a Nurse Practitioner was working in an Orange County Family Practice clinic in a barrio in Santa Ana, California. Thereafter I joined a rheumatology practice (the study and treatment of joint and inflammatory immune system diseases), ending up in a Neurology practice with a nationally well-known neurologist who specialized in headache management and chronic pain.

In the mid-70's I began studying metaphysics, ancient religions and their spiritual practices, and meditation. My first experience with meditation was as a volunteer for an experiment on meditation being conducted at UCLA. I was randomly assigned to the "meditator" group. Having no experience whatsoever, and given bare minimal instruction, I sat in the darkest room I could find and tried to "empty my mind," whatever that meant!

I found the results calming from practicing this over a few weeks period of time. I continued my own research, starting with Harvard professor, Dr. Herbert Benson's book "The Relaxation Response."

Since the early 80's I have extensively studied the then new field of psycho-neuro-immunology, now called the field of neuro-science. In addition to instructing patients on behavioral and cognitive techniques to help with pain control, anxiety and stress in the medical practice, I incorporated subtle energy medicine techniques such as acupressure, and "laying on of hands" to enhance the individual's own healing power.

Training in the traditional Western "medical model" with the professional experience of working in various medical specialties, coupled with decades of metaphysical studies and knowledge of subtle energy medicine know-how, provide a unique perspective that bridges science and spirituality.

In the late 1980's I left the medical world to help run "Power Places®," an international custom group tour company my husband Dr. Toby Weiss named and founded in the early 1980's. "Power Places®" is now a commonly used term that relates to awe-inspiring ancient sites around the world with special energies or a sense of a mystical feeling to them. Examples of such mystical sites would be the Great Pyramid and Sphinx, Machu Picchu, Stonehenge, the Mayan pyramids such as at Chichen-Itza, temples in Tibet, plus many more. He invented the special ty niche of "transformational travel," creating the mileau on-site for travelers to open their "awareness" to experience the special energies at these ancient sacred sites. As Director and Vice President I was in charge of the international on-site tours, and international conference management.

In the early 1950's I was first-born to adoring parents. They were first generation Mexican-Americans from L.A., whose parents as children or teens, fled Mexico with family members to the U.S. in the early 1900's to escape persecution during the Mexican Revolution.

I grew up in a lower middle-class Catholic traditional Mexican-American family with 7 siblings, 5 brothers and 2 sisters, plus me. The 10 of us lived in a homey three bedroom, only one bathroom house on a cul-de-sac in the quiet WASP Quaker town of Whittier, a sleepy suburb 16 miles southeast of downtown Los Angeles.

My childhood years were quite rollicking and much of the time a "fun" albeit noisy adventure. Both parents provided unconditional love and an environment of security. Yet boundaries and discipline abounded, with "respect for everyone" as a major tenet in our home. I grew up never hearing my parents even once raise their voices to each other. There was love between us siblings, although make no mistake, a war could break out if you overstayed your 6 minutes in the morning getting ready for school! I never take for granted the impact that growing up with such love, comfort and security has provided in my life.

Grandma Rosie is my maternal grandmother. And it was through her loving eyes and example that I experienced worlds beyond the 5 senses.

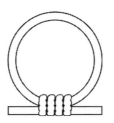

PART I

I Am a Deathwalker

Deathwalking
with Grandma Rosie

It had been an ordinary day in an ordinary week in the ordinary L.A. barrio neighborhood clinic where I worked as a Family Nurse Practitioner, except for one thing. My Grandma Rosie was dying. My Grandma Rosie, who taught me so much when I was a little girl, such as how to listen and talk to the birds. How to make mud pies, mud plates and vases. And importantly, how to add just the correct amount of tiny bits of dry twigs and dead grass to hold my miniature pottery together after it dried. Grandma Rosie, who would let me just sit and read my books in the swing downstairs on the back porch for hours and hours without calling me inside to do any chores. Grandma Rosie, who taught me how to make a perfect cup of coffee with the perfect amount of Pet "canned milk," adding just the perfect amount of sugar.

I would spend summers for a week or so at my grandparents' home. Grandma Rosie and I had a daily ritual. It was usually almost dusk and she'd sit on the front porch while I prepared her coffee. Up to that time, it was the best thing I'd ever smelled in my life. On the way back to the porch, I always sneaked a sip of that mysterious adult brew from her cup and loved it. I'd walk it out to her, and we'd sit quietly. She drinking her coffee, contemplative, and me just daydreaming. Both of us waiting for Grandpappy to come home from working at the Southern Pacific Railroad. My Grandma Rosie was dying.

Grandma Rosie, who had shared a deep mystery of life with me when I was a munchkin of about four. I had overheard an intense adult conversation. I did not understand what they were talking about nor why the adults were upset. My Grandma Rosie turned to me, looked me straight in the eye and said: "You know (pausing), there are three sides to every story ... his ... hers ... AND THE TRUTH." I had no idea at the time the meaning of what she had just said, and the multiple universal truths that statement held. Nor did I know that remembering that phrase in the years to come would, time and time again, save me a lot of pain and grief. What I did know was, at the level of my "kidhood," that what she had just told me was very important. My Grandma Rosie was dying.

A couple of years prior, Grandma Rosie had been staying with my parents and recuperating from bowel cancer surgery. She was a survivor and had a fighting spirit! As a little girl of six, Grandma Rosie, along with her mother and five brothers and sisters, had fled across the border to escape the Revolutionary War in Mexico. A short time earlier, her daddy, a white-collar government employee, had been gunned down by Pancho Villa's men while working at his office in town. He never came home from work that day, and that was that. To save her family, my great-grandmother packed up a few of their belongings and made the long trek to El Paso with her children.

As the family story goes, Grandma Rosie met Grandpappy and their romance flourished. However, Rosa's (Grandma's name in Spanish) family was not pleased with these developments. They considered Arturo Romero below Rosa's "station." Despite that, the couple moved to the L.A. area and started a new life together. Eventually, they bought property, made a home, and had three children—two boys and a girl. My beautiful mother, Norma, was the middle child.

My grandpappy worked as an electrician for Southern Pacific Railroad. He had obtained this excellent position through a non-Mexican friend who worked at the railroad yard. There was open prejudice against Mexicans, and the railroad was not likely to hire one. Grandpappy had a thin, regal nose and was very light-skinned, his paternal ancestors originally hailing from the Castilian area of Spain. He spoke excellent English, un-accented. He was proud to be self-educated, with a proud but not arrogant bearing. My first memory in life is of him taking me to the park. He'd push the swing, giving me a marvelous ride, and let me play in the sandbox as long as I wished, never rushing me. I asked Mom about this memory, and she said that had to be when I was two and a half years or so. We were living with her parents from 1951–1953, as Dad had been called to the Korean War.

One morning while Grandma was recovering from her surgery, we were sitting on the living room couch. She began talking about angels and prayers. That led to us discussing the existence of alternative ways of communication. This is commonly accepted in the Mexican and Hispanic traditional view of life and the world. For instance, when I was young, she showed me how to listen to the birds chirping and singing. What were they talking about? She showed me how to look closely at a flower. Could I "sense" anything by looking and being very still?

For sure I remember my mom telling me multiple times, as a kid, that every time she'd call Grandma, the first thing Mom would hear Grandma say was, "I was just thinking about you." Funny, the same thing would happen vice-versa when Grandma called Mom. After I moved out of my Mom's home, I'd suddenly think of Mom and for no reason, the phone would ring, and it was mom. No surprise.

Sitting there on the couch with Grandma, I asked her if she was open to experience a way to help her relax and focus healing energies on her cancer. I then shared a technique for focusing one's awareness to tap into and surround oneself with one's own healing life force energy.

At the end of the meditative experience, I leaned over and whispered into her right ear. At the time, I had no idea why I said those words to her. No idea even of what I was saying. Yet it came out as natural as could be. I whispered, "Grandma Rosie, when you think it's finally time 'TO GO,' call me. I'll go with you."

And that is exactly what happened. This is the story of what occurred when Grandma Rosie died. I escorted her to the OtherSide, and came back. I am a Deathwalker.

On that day, I was performing my usual duties as a Family Nurse Practitioner. It had been a usual hectic clinic day with an a la carte menu of ear infections, sore throats, unexplained rashes, prenatal checks, vaccinations, and the whole plethora of a busy University of California, Irvine barrio family medicine practice. It was 1982, barely in my thirties, very healthy, and my usual.

Then something odd happened. One moment, I was standing at the counter, writing in a chart of a patient I'd just finished

examining. The next moment, I developed an overwhelming feeling of sleepiness. I felt empty and heavy at the same time. All I
could think of was where I could lie down, right at that instant,
before I fell down. I stumbled into a darkened treatment room
that had a padded examination table, lay down, and felt like I
dove into a big black hole. I was not frightened, surprised, scared,
or anxious. I was surprisingly objective and matter-of-fact about
diving into this black hole.

I involuntarily exhaled deeply. That exhalation sent me flying
like Super Girl over the houses and streets to Grandma Rosie's
hospital room. It seemed only mere moments. She was standing
next to her bed, looking down at her own dead body. Her body
without vibrancy, without a pulsating presence. Her back was to
me as I walked over to what I'll call her "spirit" body.

She looked to be around her mid-to-late thirties and thinner
than I had ever seen her. She had on a long, shimmering golden
pink gown. Simultaneously, I noticed I was wearing a full-length
cape, shimmering with silver and violet hues. We were alone in the
hospital room. Placing my right hand on her left shoulder, I slowly
turned her counterclockwise to face me. On her forehead was a solid
six-pointed solid star. With my left hand, I instinctively reached for
her forehead and noticed a solid six-pointed star in the middle of my
left palm. I placed my left palm's six-pointed star to line up exactly
with her forehead star. These movements completely enveloped
both of us from head to toe within my silver-violet cape.

We started rising. Faster and faster but smooth and gentle. It
was the sensation of traveling up in an elevator, minus the stom-
ach-sinking feeling—it was a gentle "rush" up. Very soft light
filtered through my cape; however, I could not see anything. I

heard sounds and noticed smells but couldn't identify them. Being taller than her, my face was up against the side of her head. Curiously, Grandma Rosie's hair was wet but not dripping. I could smell the essence of water, if that makes sense. It was as if the molecules of water were miniature bouquets of flowers, with scents I had never encountered before.

Our gentle "up" movement stopped. I stood alone, looking around. I was at the top of some sort of flat-topped hill, sixty feet or so high and approximately half a football field in diameter. At the bottom of the hill, as far around as I could see, was very dense forest. The sky was a soft gold turquoise tinged mixture. It was so relaxing and peaceful to look at. The source of the gorgeous diffused light was not visible. In other words, no sun. The colors of everything had an amazing crystal clarity. However, there were no shadows whatsoever. The light was soothing, comforting.

Approximately twenty feet away was a beautiful opaque white bench, and Rose was sitting there. The bench glinted slightly in the light and could have been alabaster. In that moment I noticed a change, a shift in my relationship with this woman sitting on the bench. In this place, I didn't feel that incredibly close personal connection I'd had my whole life with Grandma Rosie. It was different, yet in some strange way, even deeper. There was an expansive, all-enveloping sense of being "one" with her. I don't want to sound corny; however, the energy and high frequency of this "being one" with her was almost overwhelming, yet not emotional. Very hard to explain! I will never forget the incredible sense of deep peace while I was there with her.

There I stood, my back almost touching a huge, ancient, majestic, beautiful tree, my feet very close to its gigantic roots partially sticking out of the soil. A beautiful doe with the most exquisite soft brown eyes appeared next to Rose. It gently placed its head in Rose's lap and just stared up at her. The deep quality of love for Rose emanating from that doe was something I had never witnessed. It was equivalent to all the pets in the world with all the pure love they have for their humans, directing their love to the representative human, Rose. She placed her left hand on the head of the doe.

Quietly and slowly, one by one, two by two, ten by ten, other animals started to appear until there were hundreds upon hundreds of them. Mostly birds and insects, here and there a dog, a donkey, and a cat. However, it was the birds and insects who arrived in multitudes.

Wait, that little dog I spotted in the crowd was Elmer, a Mexican Chihuahua my grandma used to dote on. She had it for years, since my mom was a teen until I was around five or six. In all the years I knew Elmer, I don't ever remember hearing him bark or make any noise, for that matter. Well, there he stood, vigilant and observant as always, keenly watching everything with a sense of intelligence I couldn't help but notice. He was waiting his turn for Rose to notice him.

I saw hummingbirds, sparrows, everyday brown birds, finches, and so many insects. It was an amazing sight. I stared at all of them. Simultaneously, I became aware that they were all telepathically communicating to Rose in their own non-audible individual "language," for want of a better word. Yet somehow, I understood them, and so did Rose. They were all saying the same thing. "Thank you!" How is it possible that a hummingbird can express deep gratitude and love, much less an insect like an ant or a gnat? And why were they all saying thank you? Was it because she had loved them all when she was alive on earth, had told them so, and had consciously acknowledged and included them in her everyday life?

The summer weeks at Grandma and Grandpappy's were the only time my beloved tribe of five brothers and two sisters weren't around. You can appreciate that being there was an incredibly special time. Their little property was a world unto itself. Sitting on the swing bench in the huge backyard that was surrounded by hills on two sides, reading my books, daydreaming, and getting a sense of myself in the wonderful silence of nature. Grandma Rosie fed the birds, gave them water, and grew lots of flowers and plants. I guess that brought the insects around.

Usually in the mornings or late afternoons, we'd be outside watering the plants and flowers to take the edge off the summer heat. To this day, the smell of wet earth is one of my favorites in the world and always brings a smile. She'd tell me the story of St. Francis and how he spoke to the animals and flowers and loved the earth almost as much as God. Then she'd call out to the different creatures in the yard, sometimes singing in a low voice or emulating their call or sound back to them.

This natural scenario had a profound effect on this little girl. It was magical, yet Grandma Rosie made it ordinary and natural. I could smell the wet earth; hear and whistle back to the birds; acknowledge the worms, caterpillars, and bees; and experience Grandma Rosie communing with them all.

Back on the white bench, next, the insects were all over her, and yet strangely, I could see through them and still see her. I noticed that the insects were in some way helping Rose "clean up." "Clean up" is the best way I can describe how they were gently, almost reverentially, plucking and consuming the dead cells of her skin.

As I look back, this function of the insects must be very important. By eating and digesting the first layer of the cells of her skin, the insects were taking in the genetic coding and information of Rose Galindo Romero, her unique "fingerprint" as a physical carbon unit of this lifetime. I was curious to see what happened next. Why did the insects do this at this moment? What purpose did it serve? Where would the insects go after visiting Rose here? Was there some grand repository of insect poop or regurgitation in this strange, beautiful place, where insects went to preserve at the cell level the "passing through" of the human who had just died?

With all the communication and activity, my physical ears only heard absolute silence. Like the most nurturing, deeply comforting, "down-to-the-bone marrow" silence I experienced when Emil, our dear friend and one of the world's leading Egyptologists, had taken me deep into one of the royal tombs in the Valley of the Kings, and we sat in absolute darkness surrounded by the Sound of Silence.

I looked over the vast throng of creatures and sensed, before I saw, someone coming over the knoll. It was Grandpappy. Boy, did he look handsome! Young, around forty, wearing a dark suit so clean and sharp it was sparkling. As he walked up to Rose, I could feel his heart. He felt very shy. He could only stare at her. She was all he wanted to see. Behind the shyness was how very much he loved her. Then I noticed a nun wearing a black-and-white habit. Who was she? There were many others; however, as my attention was so drawn to the non-humans, I did not register the other people in detail.

To the left of the crowd, I now saw a figure with a white head-piece completely covering his face. The white piece only hung down to the shoulders, thus I could tell it was a man by the clothes he wore. The tunic robe was a very dark aubergine or eggplant color. He was watching this scene but did not want to be noticed. As soon as I thought to myself, "Who is this?" I just knew it was Rose's father. I knew that whatever he said or felt toward her would be the most important thing for her. Then somehow, I realized that the man with the shroud on his head was not hiding his face because he didn't want Rose to see him, it was because he didn't want me to identify him. It seemed I knew him in my present life. Who would that be? Somehow, it would disturb the vibration of what was happening here if I recognized him.

I glanced back at Rose. In her lap lay a pink opaque soccer ball-size sphere with a bumpy texture. It began to melt into a pink, sparkling viscous liquid. The liquid moved up and down her body on its own accord, up to her face and all the way to her feet, covering her completely. It seemed to be alive. Rose washed herself all over, especially taking a long time to wash her face with this substance. Over and over again.

The viscous liquid was seeping through her clothes, but strangely her clothes did not cling to her as wet cloth would. Her gown hung in folds around her as if it were dry cloth! She then stood up and slipped out of this long gown. Underneath, she had on another. This next one she dropped to the floor, undid another gown underneath, and it, too, slipped to the floor.

All movement in the environment stopped as she undid and got out of I don't know how many garments. I lost track. She kept looking down at the garments the entire time, as if she was concentrating on something in the clothes. Sometimes, she would lift her foot one at a time to step out of the clothes. I noticed that even though she kept on dropping her "outfits," there was no pile of clothes building up at her feet. The previous one she dropped would be the only one on the ground. I lost track of the outfits after number twelve because the process started speeding up.

As the clothes were being dropped, Rose was becoming younger and smaller. I saw her as a teen, then as a young girl of seven or eight, as a girl around five and wearing a cute red plaid dress. She was smiling. She seemed to love this red plaid dress. She got smaller and smaller and smaller. Now she was a baby of around eighteen months, lying on the grass, smaller, smaller, and smaller. Smaller still, then she was a fetus, then the fetus got smaller and smaller. I did not get closer, yet I could see all this as clear as if I was only a foot away. Then I saw a ball of light, smaller, smaller, then she got smaller, cell by cell, until she was only a mass of cells! Then poof—nothing. It was as if she just turned to dust, disappearing. Of course, one cannot see a group of cells with the naked eye. How could I be standing at the huge tree and see all this so clearly when I was about twenty feet away?

Suddenly, it was completely still. I was alone. I felt myself melt into the gnarly roots of the huge tree that I had been leaning against just moments before. I relaxed into the odd feeling of moving liquid-like through those ancient roots. The musty, rich "wet earth" smell was distinctive, comforting, relaxing, hypnotic, and overpowering. Then I was in a straight chute hurling down in a controlled fall, not scary at all.

Now, back in the treatment room, I saw myself (my body) lying on the table on the other side of the room. I felt so much older and wiser than that young lady (me) lying there, and looking down, I saw I was glowing a golden color. I approached me (the young lady) on the treatment table and passed my hands over my/ her body from head to toe. My left hand on top about six inches away from her, my other hand underneath her. Oddly, that meant my glowing right hand was going right through the table. The position and movement of my hands seemed to serve to somehow realign her spine and shift her heart. My golden glow vaporized as she inhaled. I was back in myself!

When I awoke, I instantly thought "something has happened." Yet I had no memory whatsoever of what I had just experienced. The darkened room had a soft golden hue. I felt peaceful, calm, yet disoriented. I felt I had slept a week. What had happened? Then it came to me, crystal clear: "Grandma Rosie just died." Strangely, I went about my work at the clinic as if nothing had happened at all. No phone call to the hospital, to Mom, not even to Toby. Weird. I felt a big blank inside, no emotion. Zero. Classic complete denial that my beloved abuelita Rosie was dead. In the days following, I felt distant yet objective, going through the motions of getting ready for Grandma Rosie's funeral. I don't remember any call or conversation with Mom, or asking Mom how she was doing.

It was a closed casket service at the memorial Mass. The church was packed. Grandma was well-thought-of in the community, and there were many relations, the elder generation all originally from Mexico. At one point, I looked up from my pew and saw Grandma Rosie standing behind her own casket! She was surveying the people who were there. She did not speak to me nor I to her. It was as though she was looking straight through all of us. She was as aged as when she had died three days earlier. Not young like the Rose I'd experienced.

The final gathering of loved ones at a funeral, religious service, or wake is an important opportunity for the one who has died to be present for their own personal societal Deathwalk. Equally, these customs or rituals, such as the funeral or service, provides a structured event for relatives, friends, acquaintances, and colleagues to be a "witness" for that person's life. It also provides a society-sanctioned closure of that person being in this reality. It gives permission to begin the process of letting go and living without that person in the midst of this world.

Notice that I called her Rose as we were in that Deathwalking experience together. I felt a bit older than Rose. Although I looked the same as myself, Rose was a thirty- to thirty-five-years-younger version of my Grandma Rosie. I felt emotionally objective toward Rose without the personal connection and love I had with Grandma Rosie. It's difficult to describe. There was an absence of a personal, deep connection or personal love. What was present was a deep, peaceful, general sense of love, yet detached, toward another human and an overall love of humanity. In my experience in the golden world, I did not feel the presence of emotions that this was my beloved grandmother.

A few days after I wrote of this Deathwalking experience with her, I began to think that maybe it made perfect sense not to feel emotional and instead to take an objective stance; otherwise, it could possibly interfere with the experience. My desire to "hold on" to her could potentially have interfered and changed the process/experience. I was wrong.

How many times have we heard someone say when a loved

one is dying, "I just can't let him/her go," or "he/she is hanging by a thread." As a nurse who's able to function and be a facilitator, putting emotion aside at times of crisis, was I drawing on my medical background at that moment? Did this deep, peaceful sense of connectedness of being as "one" go way beyond the personal love?

The last time I saw Grandma Rosie physically alive was at the hospital the day before she died. I walked into her private room. The nurses had her sitting up high in bed. She was pretty much comatose. I just stood there and watched her breathe. It was surrealistic. The silence was stunning, the presence of Life, Death, and Beyond palpable. Unplanned and without a thought, I leaned over and whispered, "Grandma Rosie, remember to call me." I could not think of anything else to say. To this day, I wish I would have told her how much I loved her. How important she was in my life. How her house and my summertime visits were key. I don't think she knew this as she lay dying but maybe she did.

I stared at the now-tiny woman who had been a giant presence for me growing up, now shriveled up in the upright electric hospital bed. She had that gasping, harsh, irregular breathing people get when they are on their "way out." It's called Cheyne-Stokes breathing. I was immobile, staring at her, not breathing myself. I spun around and hurriedly left. I just wanted it to be over.

Downstairs at the hospital entrance, I saw my parents standing on the curb. My dad was hugging my mom while she cried. Mom always told me that Grandma Rosie was not only her mother but her best friend. In the last five years of her life, Grandma Rosie had developed some sort of organic brain syndrome and had changed personalities, especially toward Mom. All of us grandkids did not visit as much as we should have; it just wasn't much fun.

There my beloved mom was on the street with her mother/ best friend dying upstairs. I was about ten feet away and paused for a moment to look at my parents. "Are you all right?" I asked. Mom shook her head yes.

I walked to my car, got in and drove away, late for work. I am sorry, Mom, that I was not there for you in that moment.

When someone we know is dying, we get weird in various degrees, no doubt about it. Even when we don't know the person, we get weird at some level. In the West, there is not a factual acceptance of death as just a part of life. I had just said goodbye to Grandma Rosie and come down to the street to find my mom weeping. I already must have been feeling weird about it and basically just walked away. It is only in writing that all this becomes so crystal clear.

Years later, Mom told me the following story. Two days before Grandma died, my mom had gone to the hospital to visit. Grandma Rosie was awake. Mom didn't say what they talked about, and I wondered. The following day, the day before Grandma Rosie died, Mom returned, and Grandma Rosie was in a coma and non-responsive.

My mother asked, "Mom, give me a sign that you can hear me or know I am here." Grandma Rosie gave a low grunting moan.

My mom said, "It's okay to go now if you want. Dad is waiting for you." Grandma Rosie turned her head to the side, and a single tear rolled down her cheek.

Indeed, Grandma Rosie left to meet Grandpappy on the OtherSide the next day.

A Prayer for Dying and Transiting
Out of Your Body

I leave with love.
I leave in light.
I leave with heart.
I leave with mind.
I leave with will.
I leave with thanks.
I leave with no regrets.
I leave because I wish to.
I leave because it is done.
I leave with a smile.
I leave with a song.
I leave with a dance.
I leave to begin.
To begin is TO BE.

—Theresa Dominguez-Weiss

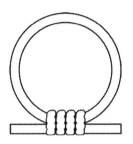

PART II

Initiations on Becoming
a Deathwalker

Stairway to Heaven on a Rope: Seventh Grade Suicide

It was in seventh grade when suicide first entered my world. I had eagerly entered the talent show at school. Being a Leo, I was sort of a "showoff" and wanted the attention from my parents and schoolmates that winning a talent show could bring. I diligently practiced my routine of a particular Mexican Folkloric dance that I had gracefully twirled through since the age of six. At dress rehearsal with the entrants and a couple of teachers in attendance, I quickly surmised that out of the many entries, two potentially stood in my way to the first-prize trophy. These previously unknown to me eighth graders, Peggy Sullivan and Joseph Cotton, posed formidable challenges. Peggy was showing off her manly Russian dancing, which was neither intricate nor as graceful as my steps. The dancing was accompanied by a cacophony of music. However, she ended her number with two cartwheels. "Big deal," I thought to myself. Cartwheels are ostentatious but there was no finesse or gracefulness to the movements. Still, I knew people tended to be dazzled by these sorts of maneuvers. I could only hope she'd be called at the beginning of the show with me toward the end.

Now Joseph's dancing was something else altogether. His ballet solo was graceful, classy, and downright riveting. When he leaped across the stage accompanied by a now-forgotten classical piece, he had everyone's full attention. Somehow, the music and leaps of gracefulness on a bare stage all combined to show most of us something we'd never seen before: a bit of uplifting classical heaven.

I'll spare you all the details of my preteen anxiety as I prepared for the big show and the day leading up to that event. As predicted, the judges were easily dazzled by the superficiality of Peggy's cartwheel. She captured that first-prize trophy. However, I did get second place and a pretty trophy, and Joseph got third. I remember watching his performance from backstage, and the effect on all the parents, teachers, and other adults in the audience. There was a strangeness and tenseness to the silence. Far from the serene, beautiful sense of being transported to another world that the kids who saw the dress rehearsal experienced.

A few days later, Joseph was dead by his own hands, with his own rope, in his own house. Word was he was gay. I sort of knew what the word "gay" meant, but not really. Just that it was "not good to be gay ..." People said he felt ashamed and made fun of. Rumors were whispered that his father and mother ... who knows. I do vaguely remember his dad looked like a sourpuss, his mom a mouse. Both with absolutely no life "spark," flat as two pieces of cardboard. I took it as a matter of fact that my parents always sparked with energy, their good looks, mannerisms, and ready smiles a magnet to all. I do know that not one single adult either at school or outside school said a peep about the suicide to us kids.

In my mind's eye, when I think of Joseph, three scenarios arise.

1. I still remember seeing him gracefully suspended up in the

air, and hearing that beautiful music during rehearsal. A "look" on his face. In that moment, he was somewhere I'd never been.

2. During rehearsal at the end of his number, the music stopped, the dancing stopped, he stopped. He stood perfectly still in his full skinny self on the naked bare stage in front of the cheap, velvet curtain. The "look" was gone. Looking over the tops of our heads, in that moment it was his eyes I'll never forget. Haunted, hurt, alone, frightened, sad ... all these flashed by in a second through his eyes. And then, there was no longer light in them.

3. When I heard he had hanged himself, all I could envision were his skinny legs in the white tights, in the middle of a small, shadowy room, hanging limp. It was beyond my twelve-year-old comprehension that someone could be in that much despair that they would use a rope to cut off their life's air supply.

In looking back, it is not hard to imagine that if any of us at school would have spoken to him with a little kindness and consideration, if we would have offered a little compassion, extended an invitation, shown a little acceptance of him, given him encouragement in his gift, expressed a few words of encouragement, perhaps, maybe, he might still be alive. I am not saying it was our fault he was depressed. We just did not make it any easier.

Adults, whether they are parents or not, need to set an example for all children. Namely, that it is not acceptable to make fun or ostracize someone who's different from us, especially those we don't understand. Tolerance makes the world go round, even before love does!

Nicknames like "Mr. Potato Head," "Olive Oil," "Skinny Minny," "Fat Butter Butt," "Volcano Face" (acne cursed), and all the other names we heard and said growing up have one purpose and one purpose only: to bully, put down, squash, keep off guard, make feel small, lord it over the other, or oppress the other. These verbal swords are used to enhance the power of those who carry a mantle of insecurity. Over the years, we fine-tune them and they just become subtler and deadlier.

Instead of saying "Nerd the Turd," why not "Rocket Man" for the kid who wants to be a space engineer? Why cannot nicknames be used to express uplifting qualities or perhaps the special attributes that parents may wish to cultivate or be present in the life of their child? For example, take a look at Native American or Oriental names. "She Who Knows the Wind" (think of everything the wind brings, seeds for planting, birds, rain); "Moon Daughter" (reflects the light of others, implies knowledge and understanding of the hidden and deep emotions of others, subdued); "He Who Dances with Wolves" (conveys an important aspect of Kevin Costner's character in the film).

What is suicide? It is the taking of one's life. Although a huge step down from the literal "final act," we all commit suicide in some way frequently during our daily lives. There's not really such a quantum difference between putting a rope around your neck and kicking away from a chair, and driving around in a car when you're thinking you would like to kill a particular person, or daring the next guy to cut in front of you. Or snorting coke every day, making you lax in your responsibilities. Or screaming at or smacking your children, taking out on them what you are inside really upset about. Or getting drunk every day and denying it. Or being drawn to one abusive relationship after another, or worse, staying in an abusive relationship. Keeping hate in your "gut" for your ex, and leaking out that hate to the children you both share.

Spewing negativity to someone who's harmed you. Spreading malicious gossip which you think makes you superior. Looking in the mirror and going through a check-off list of everything you see that you hate about yourself or think is wrong with yourself.

We place the blame of our slow "suicide" on others. We categorize it with names like change, transition, restructuring, PMS, pre-menopause, midlife crisis, "my nerves," sleeping problem, my husband, my wife, my "ex," my teenager, my mother, my father, my childhood, my office associate, my boss, my twenty-first birthday, my thirtieth, my fortieth, my fiftieth, my sixtieth, my seventieth birthday, my in-laws, my neighborhood, my income, my career, my country, the world, another nationality, global change, politics, genetically engineered food, terrorism, crazy people, chemicalized water, poisoned food supply.

We lay this mantle of "blame" for the fact that we cannot deal with living our lives. And our anxiety just keeps our wheels spinning, our denial denying, and our self-loathing singing a litany of unhappiness in the recesses of our psyche.

Are not all these cause-and-effect actions a very, very slow or not-so-slow internal suicide in some way? All these actions chip away our enthusiasm, our "light" for living; they take away living in peace, joy, and contentment.

Joseph looked around and made his choice. If suicide offered him a way out, I only hope that wherever he is now, he's got that "look" on his face while dancing.

Thank you, "He Who Shows Us Heaven," for sharing moments of "true grace" doing what you loved.

Dr. Kübler-Ross Cracks
Open My Universe

At age nineteen while working as a nurse at Rancho Los Amigos Hospital, I cared for kids who had sustained catastrophic spinal cord injuries. Many were paraplegic, and they were the lucky ones. Some were on breathing machines with a hole in their throat for the tube to pass through. A darling young boy of seven had to live at least sixteen hours a day in a chamber to compress his chest in order to force the air out, and then fill the lungs back up during a mechanical inhalation.

For others, their only voluntary movement was to blink! These were the quadriplegic kids. They couldn't even swallow their own saliva, as their spinal injury was so high up in the neck next to the base of the skull that it knocked out the instinctive ability to even take a breath.

I loved working with these kids. You would think they would be depressed and their moods somber. However, it was as if we were in a macabre summer camp. The kids enjoyed the fact that they were living, dorm-style, two to six kids in a room. They just hung out and kidded and sometimes fought with each other.

Parents were not around except when they visited on the weekends (most kids were from out of town and even some from out of the country). School was on the hospital grounds. What I did not realize in my naiveté was that the ramifications of their injuries, for the most part, had not truly sunk into their mindset.

The kids came to this unit for long-term rehabilitation after acute hospitalization subsequent to their accidents. Ninety percent were boys, full of life, active, bright, "full of promise" kids, who had their spinal cords severed because of diving off cliffs, motorcycle accidents, playing football, or such activities. Most were hopeful and optimistic.

Due to my medical training, I was acutely aware of the probable outcome in store for these darling boys and young men. I chose to favor an unrealistic hope that these mere "youths" would eventually overcome their catastrophic probability of succumbing to an early death. Now I realize that perspective allowed me to walk into their rooms every day, enthusiastic and optimistic with a real sense of hope.

In some ways, many of these kids were the "non-walking dead." I did not realize it at the time. My age, sometimes a mere year or two more than theirs, brought their "living death" close to home in an unguarded moment. In looking back, I call these young people who are profoundly injured, like being paraplegic or quadriplegic, the "living non-walking dead." In our youth, we all thought that somehow, because their whole lives were still in front of them, they would miraculously get better. Against all odds. Months would go by as they continued their rehab. Gradually, the light would fade from their eyes until one day, there was no spark. I refused to see that the spark was gone in any one of those kids.

I had to refuse to see, or there was no way I could walk in every day, smile with them, cut up their food, spoon-feed them, change their urinary catheters, and tell them stories about my growing up in a large Mexican American family just outside of East L.A.

Into this hospital world, the world-famous psychiatrist Elisabeth Kübler-Ross came to deliver her seminar. Around twenty of us hospital staff had signed up for this workshop on "cancer, death, and dying with children." I am not sure why I took this workshop because I did not work with cancer patients. However, what I would hear would brand my brain for life.

That morning, the workshop attendees milled around, quiet and shy and expectant as strangers are when gathered together in a room for the same purpose. Sipping coffee and mostly glancing at the floor, I probably did not say much to anyone.

Suddenly, this small woman, powerful, and obviously on a mission, strode into the room. I could only stare at her, mesmerized. A magnetic presence emanated from her as she scanned the room, her owlish huge glasses reflecting the soft light. Even before she started to speak, I found myself moving to the front of the room and plopping myself right in front of her.

Over the next few hours, I heard revolutionary news, at least for me. Those children who had terminal illnesses and faced death could actually talk about death, sing about it, cry about it, and very movingly draw pictures about it. All so much easier than adults. They were so much wiser and more accepting of what was happening to them than the adults.

Dr. Kübler-Ross spoke with such passion and conviction. She had obviously been inspired by these dying children. On a large whiteboard, she drew wonderful pictures for us that the children had drawn as they talked about what was happening to them. I still remember a story about a boy and a dove that he drew. Not the details, but I could sense that this one had really "grabbed" her.

This day with Dr. Kübler-Ross imprinted me in many ways that I realize only now as I write this book. I was working with pediatric quadriplegic and paraplegic children, the "living non-walking dying and dead" on the teen ward. Their ultimate outcome of death by some aspect of organ breakdown or infection, way before their time if they would have had intact bodies.

And then there was the possibility of severe depression, begging the answer to the ultimate question. What is the point … what is the point of living?

I particularly remember a handsome, bright, charismatic guy of sixteen, quarterback on his team. He became a quadriplegic from a football injury. He only had the use of his tongue and one of his thumbs. With a special switch rigged to his electric wheelchair, he could manipulate his own transportation with his tongue.

Within two years of going home from the hospital, he committed suicide by driving his electric wheelchair into his pool. In my youth, I could not understand this at the time. He was from an upper middle class loving family, secure at home after discharge, with full-time medical care. What happened?

Was the last thought on his mind the ultimate question … "What is the point?" In his overwhelming psychic and mental pain and angst, he would not know that that very question had been posed millions upon millions of times throughout the millennia by people from all walks of life and circumstances.

"Man finds meaning in the face of suffering," said Dr. Viktor

Frankl, world-renowned Viennese psychiatrist, concentration camp survivor, and founder of the School of Logotherapy. Without a meaningful life, it is easy to emotionally check out. That holds true for those of us who are no longer children. Small children do not have to find meaning in the face of suffering. Life and living is beyond meaningful. Life and living *just is*. Small children are in the "flow of life," they live "in the moment," so meaning is superfluous. That is the case until inevitably comes the day when an event or events snatch the "in-the-moment" flow of life away. That state is no longer the normal. Usually, an adult is involved somehow in those snatch away scenarios.

Dr. Kübler-Ross showed us that with young dying children, there is an inherent acceptance of death. Are they not afraid to leave life? Maybe not. They have not invested a lot of time in life, so perhaps for them there is not as much to lose. They are more afraid of making their parents sad and cry, or not seeing their parents again, than they are of dying.

Years later, I realized that taking care of handicapped or dying children provided lessons to me for living a "meaningful" life. And not taking life for granted.

Children naturally go with the flow of daily life. It's like breathing to them, they don't think about it, they just "live" it.

Children dying shows us true courage and bravery.

Children dying makes us remember ourselves as children. We smile, resurrecting happy childhood memories.

Children dying forces us to regurgitate painful childhood episodes that most prefer to remain buried.

Children dying forces us to admit how much we have died inside since we were children, and we weep, grieving for our lost chances. Deep down, we cry that we have allowed ourselves to be robbed of a meaningful life using our past as an excuse.

Children dying make us pause to observe a bird building a nest where previously we would have rushed right by.

Tata: "El Rey" Without His Queen Slips Away

Tata, my paternal grandfather, was dying of prostate cancer. I had not visited him since the diagnosis. His "Sweeta," our beloved Grandma Panchita, mother of his ten sons, had passed only a couple of years earlier. The loss had brought him to his knees. Quickly and silently, he crumbled, the cancer trigger in his body taking full advantage of his suppressed immune system. Now, I walked into their home that was filled with wonderfully exciting, happy and fun childhood memories.

Their bedroom was being visited by Death ... I wasn't quite sure if its foot was just in the door, or if Death had taken up residence.

Going through the doorway of the bedroom was like walking through jello. He was lying flat on his back, pale white, and frail looking, like those who have no hope left. I did not know what to say. I had never known what to say to the great legendary patriarch of our large Mexican, now into the second generation Mexican-American, family. He ruled, he was the king, "El Rey," whom all revolved around. I'd never been alone in a room with him, much less had a private conversation. I slunk to a chair in the corner and sat. Tongue-tied, for some reason scared, and feeling very awkward. Time stopped. I was waiting for his lead. I waited, and I waited.

Later on, I found out he was on a steel bedpan when I came in the room. With his wasting-away buttocks, prostate pain, and having the rim of the bedpan cut into his butt, no wonder he wasn't talking! How could this proud, handsome man from Mexico, who came over to the U.S. as a peon to escape the miseries of the just-beginning rumblings of the deadly 1912 civil war in Mexico to make a life, tell his oldest grandchild something as private as that he was in the middle of trying to have a bowel movement? I, in turn, was overwhelmed by the whole scenario and did not say a word.

After a while, I got up and said, "I'll be going now, Tata." I touched his feet covered with the bed sheet and left. That's the last time I ever saw him.

Except whenever I watch old Westerns. My grandfather was a well-regarded character actor in the forties and fifties. Tata made movies with and hung out with John Wayne, Wallace Beery, Anthony Quinn, and was even in a movie with Frank Sinatra. As kids, my siblings and I would watch old Westerns on Saturday mornings before our parents woke up. We would look for Tata in the foreground or in a scene with John Wayne. "There's Tata!" we would all shout when inevitably we spotted him. I still say that out loud, just as when we were kids, whenever I spot him while watching an old Western.

"El Rey," from immigrant to successful, well-regarded Mexican actor—in those days, a rarity in Hollywood cinema. What a legend …

"Tata, te amo. Estas en paz"

Little Mary, Gone in a Blink

My first real nursing job at the tender age of nineteen was as a Licensed Vocational Nurse in the Pediatric Unit at Rancho Los Amigos in Downey, California. Children from two months old to teenagers with spinal cord injuries, birth defects, neurological disorders, polio, and a myriad of devastating injuries and diseases came from all over the world to "Rancho," a pioneering, world-renowned rehabilitation hospital. In 1969, Rancho was different from other hospitals because of the acute levels of injuries they admitted, cared for, and rehabilitated right out of intensive care units.

These children could be hospitalized from two months to sometimes more than two years. The medical issues and/or injuries were acute or chronic, catastrophic, and always overwhelming to the child and their families. That is, if they had a family. The nursing staff gave these poor unfortunates love and compassion in addition to highly skilled, world-class nursing care. We made the units homey to reflect a family setting as much as possible.

In the summer of 1970, I was on the unit that handled infants and young children up to ten years old. We received a call that a five-year-old female with a "C2" injury would arrive shortly.

She had fallen out of a tree she'd been climbing and broken her neck. It was unusual that she was still alive with such a high neck injury. That means her neck fracture was at the second cervical vertebra, literally where your brain attaches to your spinal cord. An injury that high pretty much means the only thing you can do is blink, make facial movements, and maybe move your head from side to side. If you are lucky, you can somewhat swallow and chew. Injured at this high level, you can't breathe on your own. Unless high-quality emergency care is provided quickly at the scene of the accident, you're a goner. Christopher Reeves of "Superman" fame is an example of this type of high cervical injury.

From the beginning, Mary was the darling of the unit for me. She was so cute, a real doll, tanned, huge brown sparkling eyes, a dazzling perfectly white smile, sandy blond hair in a tomboyish "bob" cut, intelligent, saucy, impish, and full of life. Her parents were attractive, in their early thirties, upper middle class, well-educated WASPS from ritzy, horsy Palos Verdes, California. They were crazy about Mary, and she was crazy about them.

From Day One, I was smitten with Mary. I always wanted her assigned as one of my patients and successfully maneuvered it to be so. Each day would start off the same. First thing, I'd have to put on her stereo to play her favorite rock group, Creedence Clearwater Revival (CCR). To their rollicking music, I'd brush her teeth, wash her from head to toe, and comb her hair. Her morning ablutions always ended with me gently scratching the back of her neck. She just loved that and always begged for more, making the cutest face.

She was on a respirator, a breathing machine, full time. This means she was not capable of taking one breath in on her own volition. She had a tracheotomy tube sticking out of a hole in her throat, and the tube was attached to the respirator. A tracheotomy frequently collects mucous secretions and fluid inside. This necessitated the airway being suctioned with a skinny catheter tube put down the tracheotomy and into her throat, while a suction machine drew out the mucous secretions. The difficulty is that the person undergoing this experience feels as if all the air is being sucked right out of them. It feels like you are suffocating. Imagine being five years old and every half hour or so, you have to go through being suffocated and you can't move a muscle! You can only trust.

It is hard to write this story of Mary. I was only 20 at the time, and she was the first person I ever witnessed die right in front of my eyes. As I write this over twenty years later, I can still clearly see her hair, her cute little hands, the tan line from her bathing suit, her sparkly eyes. Back then, in my naiveté, I did not realize how much I loved Mary. I was just her nurse. We fit together. I knew what made her comfortable and how to make her smile, and how she liked her cereal.

No doubt, I spoiled her rotten. She knew it, I knew it, we didn't care, and we had a great time together. We both loved life so much. We just stayed "in the moment," and never indicated to each other what "might" happen later. Her mom seemed to appreciate the fact that we were dealing with only one week to a month in advance at a time. The family understandably was still in shock as was Mary herself. The full impact had not sunk in yet.

I was very aware that Mary thought this was a temporary situation. Somewhere inside, she decided she would play "this game" very well. And so she did. How does a five-year-old comprehend not ever climbing a tree again and certainly not being able to even feel one?

The songs and music of Creedence Clearwater Revival were magic for her. They never failed to work their charm. No matter what was happening, how uncomfortable she became with the involuntary leg spasms that jolted her entire precious little body, or not being able to do one thing for herself but lie there. If you wanted her to snap out of being contentious or stubborn, and she did have a stubborn streak a mile wide (hmm, reminded me of someone I knew—myself), CCR worked instantaneously to make her eyes dance. One of her favorites was "Down on the Corner." "…Willy and the poor boys are playing … bring a nickel … tap your feet …" She'd dance by shrugging her shoulders to the music. The rhythm was just the right tempo to allow her to sing on exhalation. How could she sing if she had a tube in her throat and was on a respirator? During the exhalation phase of the respirator, she'd breathe out. That's how I knew her voice.

I was mesmerized by Mary's happiness, sparkling eyes, great courage, and yes, total complete absolute denial and five-year-old incomprehension of what the future would bring. A life that professionally I knew would probably be a very short one. A life of only being able to blink, smile, and barely swallow, and having to be very careful at that. A life where she only could be heard on exhalation. We loved gabbing together, easily getting into the flow of exhalation speech. Mary had an opinion about everything, even when she was not asked! Kinda funny, as that is how I was.

Mary's parents had an attitude of denial, like this was a temporary situation. Otherwise, how could Mary's mom possibly go on, knowing that Mary, her unique, one-of-a-kind, precious gift from God, was permanently broken and smashed? Like a priceless Ming vase shattered in an earthquake.

Mary's condition eventually stabilized. With intensive training and rehabilitation, it got to the point that finally she could begin home visits for the weekends. This was a big thing, an ordeal taking an inordinate amount of preparation. In those days, it took weeks to get an electric wheelchair custom-fit to her precious little body. There had to be room at the back of the wheelchair for a portable respirator and all necessary emergency and suction equipment. The family van was converted with an electric ramp to lift the wheelchair to be able to roll it inside the van.

Mary's parents were trained and drilled in all her nursing care, hygiene needs, emergency techniques, how to feed her, and how to suction her to keep the secretions from choking her. They now knew how to turn her so she wouldn't get bed sores, how to roll the towels/pads with a sheepskin on top perfectly under her tiny bottom in her wheelchair so that when she was lifted back to bed, her little "booty" would not have even one tiny red speck, her body weight would have been so perfectly distributed.

Imagine teaching a mother how to take care of her own baby. This time, a mistake or back turned for a second, and her baby could be dead in that second. In many ways, Mary was more vulnerable than a newborn.

But Mary wasn't a newborn. She'd been with her parents and family for five years, plus the nine months of "uterus residence." Five years is plenty of time to pack in a lot of memories, living, and enjoying life as a family. It is normal for any parent to expect they will have the rest of their lives to be with their child. I suspect that most parents don't even think about it; it is something they take for granted, and they should take for granted. It is the natural order of things.

Surely Mary's parents took it for granted. They had Mary and I believe two other children. Mary's parents were young, good-looking, smart, successful, and seemed to be in love with each other. They lived in the "right" area, were moneyed, and had some privilege … They were living a successful American family dream. That is, until Mary fell out of the tree the summer of 1970.

The Saturday morning finally arrived that Mary was going home for her first weekend. Her mom came in looking calm, organized, and totally together as usual, from her Ralph Lauren freshly starched oxford shirt and imported Italian loafers to the take-charge yet compassionate look on her face. Looking back, no question, she had to have been terrified inside. In order to function to take care of her Mary, she had to put the lid on her anxiety and fear at a really deep level. She was a brave, courageous, beautiful, golden lioness come to pick up her cub. She was fiercely dedicated to protecting her offspring and keeping her family unit together.

I had all of Mary's gear and medical paraphernalia packed up and ready to go. Mary was absolutely ecstatic. She was going home! It had been months since her accident, and she'd been in this "other world" reality. This morning, her "real" world would shortly be surrounding her once again. I held myself back and just looked on as I let her mother roll her into the canvas sling and then put her in the wheelchair with the use of a stainless steel bedside crane that lifted Mary out of bed and into the wheelchair. She then switched Mary over to her portable respirator.

I felt anxious. How could I possibly convey all of Mary's nuances of medical care, all her signals and signs when she was wanting something, to her mom? I could anticipate her next want and need, most of the time, before Mary even knew it! In my twenty-year-old naiveté, I did not realize that Mary was this golden lioness's baby girl. She knew her baby cub better than I ever would, medical necessities or not. She knew what her crushed cub's desires, wants, and needs would be. As a mother, she was an expert in her kid's cryptic code of communication and sometimes just blatant stubbornness, and how to handle it.

Out the door went Mary's entourage. Her brother, Mary's big doll, and mom's friend, all to the cocoa brown van with the hydraulic lift platform. All were silent as her mom rolled Mary onto the hydraulic lift. The switch was thrown and the only sound was the whirs of the machine as the hydraulic lift noise mixed with the click of Mary's breathing machine on the platform taking Mary up. Her mom pulled her off the platform into the van, and the door was slammed shut. She hopped in the driver's seat, and with everyone waving goodbye, except for Mary, they drove off. I went back to the room to make her bed. Without Mary's machines hissing and whirring, the quiet was beyond my comfort zone. I missed her.

I remember that day's shift as being a long one. It became clear how much I would always want to be around Mary now that there was just her empty bed. Underlying this weekend sojourn was a huge, obvious medical care issue. How they fared this weekend would portend Mary's future, as she'd eventually have to be discharged from this rehabilitative hospital. No one wanted to see this kid institutionalized with only weekend home visits. On the other hand, how could a single family unit take the chronic stress of managing the twenty-four-hour care of someone like Mary, who was 100 percent dependent and would not grow out of it, like a newborn eventually does?

Sunday afternoon arrived, and Mary, Mom, and neighbor

returned. I was the first one to see her as she came rolling down the hall. The commotion was comforting as the bells and whistles and whooshing of the respirator all got turned back on at the bedside as Mary was lifted up and put back to bed. Mom looked tired and wiped; Mary was frayed around the edges. Both seemed to breathe a sigh of relief, or was it my imagination?

It must have been difficult for Mary's mom to leave her baby again. I was impressed, once again, by how courageous this mother lioness was. I would watch over Mary for her until the next home visit, and I would love doing it. On went CCR as I knew the music would distract Mary and help ease the transition back to this other reality.

It is quite shocking the first time someone goes home from the hospital after that person has had a horrendous, devastating physical trauma, such as Mary had undergone. Up to that point, there had been various peaks and valleys of physical and emotional stabilization and weathering of the "storm," so to speak. Then a certain comfort level, an adaptation level, hopefully comes into play. The person finds their place in this hospital world. At this world-renowned orthopedic rehabilitation hospital, Mary was in a world where she fit right in. She could be wheeled around, and wherever she went within the vast acreage of this huge medical complex, she was surrounded by others who had been catastrophically crushed in some way too.

Stepping back into the other reality, her "home world," is emotionally and mentally rattling. The reality of the lifetime physical limitations hits one like a ton of bricks on so many levels. In my experience, most never quite make it out from under the ton of bricks.

I never spoke to Mary about her weekend. On looking back, that's odd on the one hand, and on the other hand, it was in keeping with our style and routine together. We never talked about the other world, the home world. Mary and I only existed in the hospital world. This was unusual for me, professionally. Part of what I was trained to do as a rehabilitation nurse is to assist the patient to integrate back into what was their world. Integrating the accident, the hospital world, and now with the return to home and the limitations and differences staring them in the face. They are a handicap in a non-handicap world. I went beyond professionalism with Mary. I loved her too much.

Here I was at twenty, naïve and open-hearted, and this kid just comes flying into my life, grabs me by the throat, and throws her arms around my heart ... I was defenseless. Talk about chemistry. I swear we shared some molecules somewhere.

I cannot recall how much time went by between Mary starting to bridge back to her Palos Verdes eucalyptus-tree neighborhood "old world," and the day she died. "The day she died." Sounds so final. In actuality, it all happened very quickly, within a few short moments. It is only in the writing of this story about my Mary that I've come to realize how painful it was for me. That I mentally, psychologically, and emotionally never processed the pain. I just completely blocked it out.

The morning Mary died started out just like all the other mornings in the hospital. Getting the kids up, brushing teeth, bathing, strapping braces on, getting after those who were lollygagging. It was a Saturday and the kids were happy there was no school. The nursing staff knew we'd have our hands full all day long! I don't remember if Mary was scheduled to go home that weekend or not. CCR was on, I fed Mary, suctioned her. I was always not more than fifteen feet away; my radar included seeing her out of the back of my head. She was in bed, PJs on, breakfast finished. It was around 10:30 a.m.

I was standing on the right, at the head of her bed, looking down at her. We were gabbing and having a good time as usual, she chatting away on exhalation.

The next second, she was just staring straight at me. Her color became paler by the second. The respirator alarm incessantly buzzed, the cue for obstructed airway. I immediately responded by doing all the things I was professionally trained to do in emergency CPR with spinal cord-injured patients. Suction, check trachea, check response level, check pupils, check respirator, and use a bag to breathe for the patient in case of possible mechanical failure. Within just a few seconds, other nursing staff were there in response to my shout for assistance. Nothing worked, she just stared, her pupils quickly fixed and dilated. One of the signs of brain death.

I had been bagging her (a medical term for when you take a person off a mechanical respirator assist device and hook up the squeezable bag directly to the tube in the patient's throat). It meant she was getting oxygen to her lungs, as I could see her chest rising and falling. One can pump/squeeze/blow oxygen in a rhythmic fashion.

Her tiny chest rhythmically moving up and down did nothing to pink up her skin color. To check to see if she would respond to pain, I dug my fingernail into the tiny indented space on her top lip between the bottom of her nostrils and the top of her upper lip to check for a response. NONE. Her pupils just became more dilated.

Dr. Perry, the Medical Director of Pediatrics, was on the scene in a few minutes. He said based on what I told him and how quickly things happened, Mary probably threw a blood clot to her brain. Massive stroke or internal brain bleed. At least that is what I think I heard him say. Ocean waves were pounding in my head. He pronounced her dead.

I took one last look at her. I turned on my heel and walked quickly to the staff restroom down the hall. I leaned over the toilet to puke but the vomit was stuck in my stomach. I could barely breathe; my throat was clamped shut. My head felt like a truck had smashed into it, splattering my brain matter like a ripe melon. With each hyperventilating breath, my mind screamed, "No," "No," "No," "No," "No," "No," like a broken record. I was in the bathroom for I don't know how long, paralyzed. A million shards of glass shredding my heart, mind, and soul.

These types of symptoms/reactions are commonly known as "shock syndrome," when one is confronted with a sudden, devastating moment. The brain is attempting to compute the information. It has suddenly released a flood of chemicals that are saturating the cognitive centers too quickly for the mind "to make sense" out of the sensory input.

Sitting down, I stared at the floor under the toilet. To this day, I can describe to you exactly what the tile looked like, the door, the toilet, the walls, and how cold the air was. I went to the sink to wash my face and hands. I could not, would not, look in the mirror. I did not want to look into my eyes.

Eventually, I walked out to the nursing station. Dr. Perry kindly told me there was nothing more anyone could have done. Mary was not in distress when she died. I worked the rest of my shift. I functioned. Internally, I was completely shut down, and each minute, I buried it deeper. I don't remember that I ever mentioned one thing to anyone, that day or since.

I'm sure my co-workers probably asked me how I was doing but I don't remember. For a while, I couldn't look anyone in the eye. What added to the trauma was the suddenness. One minute Mary was there; the next minute literally she was gone. It was as if her consciousness, her spirit, just gathered her all up in one moment and zipped off to wherever the "cosmic transit lounge" is.

Mary's was the first death I'd ever witnessed. Since then I have observed many go through the process of dying, but in a gradual, slow way. In that gradual process there appears to be a cell by cell, molecule by molecule life energy disconnect that takes place. From the literal physical standpoint, this would correlate with the body slowly starting to shut itself down. A transition process. In some deaths, the "life force" slowly disconnects its trillions of cells. The person seems to have one toe, or foot, in the world of the living, and the other in the other realm of existence or non-existence.

Mary's is the only death I have been present for that was instantaneous. It was as if the "Angel of Death" came and just snipped her cord, disconnecting her life energy and conscious-ness, and just zapped her away in an instant. Immediately after she died, her "essence" wasn't around at all; the sense of her pres-ence vanished. There was nothing, no energy, nothing palpable at all, such as I've experienced in every other death I've ever been around since that day.

It was as if the disconnect of the trillions of cells that I have experienced in all the other deaths I've witnessed occurred with Mary in a completely different way. Perhaps with her, the disconnect had begun when she had her accident, making the exit faster because she was already so disconnected. Neurologically, her brain was disconnected from her spinal cord and thus her entire body in many ways. Whatever the reason or reasons were, when her moment came, she was free from this reality. Quickly and neatly … literally in the blink of an eye. Maybe it was just time, maybe it just was.

I never got to say goodbye to Mary. Never told her how I felt. I loved you so much, Mary.

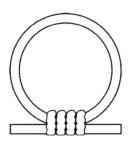

PART III

Metamorphic Life Experiences

Our Pets: Treasures of True Love

Barnaby and me. It's been many years since Barnaby made the transit to "feather heaven," as I semi-jokingly say. As I wrote the words "Barnaby and me," it surprised me how emotional I felt and how I developed a tight spot in my heart. Barnaby was a cockatiel given to me by a family practice doctor friend in the early eighties. Barnaby was gorgeous, cocky, observant, very independent and smart, curious and full of life. His satiny dove gray feathered coat was topped off by a yellow sun on each cheek, centered by a brilliant orange spot. His top notch feathers were snow white, as was the part of his face around his nose and throat. He was a baby when I got him, and from the beginning, that bird was in my heart. I'd talk to him in the morning first thing, and he was the first one to tweet hello when I arrived home.

He was stubborn, and like a cat, would call the shots on when it was allowed to give or receive signs of affection. I kept on wishing he'd sing more. Even if I'd sit and imitate a cockatiel song, he'd make a few teasing sounds back to me as if he were going to sing, but he wouldn't. However, when he chose to sing, it was glorious.

I loved it. For some reason, it made me so happy. I just wanted him to sing all the time.

He also fought me on easily coming to me and letting me pet him or touch him. No matter the amount of coaxing, he would not sit on my finger when I'd put my hand in his cage. I'd have to wait and wait until he came out, and with my fingers crimped, he'd perch on my curved index finger.

I absolutely loved it when he was perched on my shoulder as I walked around the house. In the kitchen, I'd be cooking and he'd be walking around the floor. It was weird that I always knew exactly where he was and never stepped on him, even when he was silently right behind me or under my feet.

Our relationship was pure and uncomplicated, no strings attached. He was there when I wanted him, and he never bugged me or demanded one thing from me. I did wish, however, that he'd jump on my finger and want to be closer with me, like the relationship my friend Carlene had with her cockatiel.

One of my most precious moments with Barnaby was the only time he flew over and stood on my chest while I was lying on the couch. He came waltzing up to my face, and with the greatest tenderness "kissed" me, actually repeatedly pecking me all over my mouth and lower cheeks.

As pets do, Barnaby became my alter ego. He would only make his irritating "squeaky door" sound when Toby and I would have an argument, as is normal in marriage. I swear Barnaby knew his "squeaky door" sound bugged Toby to no end.

My personal and professional life became very busy and demanding, and with those demands, I felt a lot of stress. In late 1989, I crashed into the "dark night of my soul," or as I call it …

nuclear meltdown, my "China Syndrome,"... otherwise known as a midlife crisis. I went from working out, being very active, feeling upbeat, thinking positively, looking at the bright side of things, and thinking "everyone is beautiful in their own way" — to a withdrawn, depressed, and gloomy person with an all-pervading sense of hopelessness and futility.

In short, I went to bed and couldn't get up. I was deliberately disconnected from everyone and everything. Even when someone attempted contact, like my beloved husband, Toby, I just couldn't respond — I felt nothing. I was as dead as a bleached-out piece of driftwood in the Sahara Desert. Certainly in life, it is normal to have episodes of feeling distant at times with a member of the family, some friends, the career, co-workers, the neighborhood where one lives, or whatever. I think I have made my point. Some people even get disconnected or maybe were never even connected to God, the Creator, or whatever name people use to designate the Divine.

For various reasons, in my life I had at times distanced myself from individuals, places, and things, either temporarily, long-term, or permanently. This is part of the ebb and flow of life. However, I always, no matter what, felt contact with Divine Spirit or whatever word you wish to use. Now I was off in this dark hole, alone and by choice. I did not care, leave me alone, I do not need your help. Anger was nowhere to be seen or felt. I was slow-motion swimming in a dark, bottomless dry ocean (makes no sense, how can the ocean be dry, but … there it is). I could not feel God; I could not feel the connection with Father/Mother God. It was a complete nothingness/void. Never in my life did I not feel God or the thread of the Holy Spirit. Not feeling connected was the absolute worst part for me. I was a blank slate of nothingness. This included not relating to Toby, my stepdaughter Rebecca, family nor Barnaby.

I'd go through the motions of the day, sometimes. Other times, the furthest I made it was to the living room to stare out the window at the ocean off in the distance. Toby asked me if I wanted to take a year off from our Power Places®' office. I did not say no but I did not say yes either. I just stopped going to work.

I was too depressed to feel grateful. I only could play the head tapes of "How can I not work" (meaning: then who am I?). "How can I let Toby just work? I am capable and professional and have been taking care of my financial needs since I was fifteen" (meaning: I don't need a man to take care of me). "If I don't work, that means I am weak and needy" (meaning: my whole life I got to where I am by pushing and doing it all myself). "Weak and needy are not applauded or admired."

Did I take advantage of the first year off since I was fifteen to do creative projects, practice to get in shape for a marathon, or read the books I'd wanted to read for years? Did I take the time to go sit at sidewalk cafes in Laguna and observe and enjoy the beach scene, or go window shopping? NO. I just sat there, too sucked dry of energy and feeling to move. I ignored Barnaby and everything else, and sometimes I did not even change his water. Sometimes I forgot to take the cover off his cage until the afternoon time. I was in a funk of a fog for sure.

Previous to that, Barnaby had an array of sounds, squeaks, and chirps. I enjoyed hearing his welcome-home notes before I even got to the driveway. How did he know it was me coming down the street? I came home always calling out inside to myself, "I'm home." This was something in me leftover from childhood when I'd come running home from school, throw open the door, say "I'm home," and there would be my beloved Mamacita. Hopefully, with some freshly made arroz con leche. To this day, it's still my favorite comfort food.

In my fog of a funk that year of 1990, I gradually stopped plugging into Barnaby, you know, inter-relating. I am ashamed to say there were many times I waited way too long to change the paper at the bottom of his cage. I cried more that year than I ever did in my entire life. Barnaby sang less and less until he just stopped. In my funk of a fog depression, I never even registered the fact that he was now silent. I was blank inside and he was just one more chore to have to take care of.

Not being able to get out of bed anyway, I did not go to work for the next 11 months. Now, there was a part of me (a thin, rational part) that rubbed her hands together and said, "Yippee!" I now had free time to take art classes, to just wake up in the morning with a blank slate and ask the ultimate delicious and decadent question, without anything scheduled for the day and with an exquisite sense of anticipation: "what am I going to do today?"

I couldn't get into it and so I added to my psychological drama by getting on my case that I was not enjoying a whit this gift of a lifetime from my hubby. I said to myself, "You've been handed this on a silver platter, so damn it you better enjoy it and have fun! Do you know how many women would give their augmented right breast to have a man who is totally crazy about them, adores them, never looks at other women and says so sweet and loving, "Here's a year or more off if you want. You don't have to do anything, no strings attached, no ill will, no expectations. Do what you want."

What kind of ungrateful, weird person, given one of the biggest gifts of life, couldn't even move? I missed out on enjoying the freedom.

I was out of it, in "China Syndrome," as a woman, as a person, emotionally, mentally, psychically, and spiritually. (China Syndrome is the term for a severe-level nuclear accident causing a core meltdown that theoretically could burn a hole through the earth, making its way to the other side of the world.) As I observed my core meltdown or "Dark Night of the Soul" that has been commented on in literature for millennia, I didn't have a clue nor did I care what would happen when "China" (the other side) was actually reached. Would I experience an explosion that would send me reeling into madness?

To be honest, I never even thought about the end because I felt I'd be in this black pit of "nothing matters" from now on, and that was that. As a child, yet old enough to objectively notice people, I had surmised that adults generally fall into categories. The "alive-alive" category would be like my parents. There were those "alive-dead." The "alive-dead" fell into two categories.

Category 1: Those who are haunted by "what could have been" and have no light coming from their eyes.

Category 2: Those who have light coming from their eyeballs. However, it is not even twenty-five watts' worth when you look into their face and into their eyes. That is if they let you look into their eyes.

As I observed my depression, I figured once my fall into the black hole of "WHAT IS THE POINT OF ANYTHING" was finished, I would officially go from the alive-alive category to the alive-dead category. I started mourning the fact that I was only forty, still so young, and that to no longer be in the alive-alive category was indeed very sad. It was hard to believe that after all my adventures, the love I had in my life, my husband and family, that I was now facing the possibility of moving into the alive-dead category, halfway between haunted and rigor mortis.

And so it came to pass that during this time, Barnaby just keeled over and died. Now a little bird dying is one thing, but that his life and death would be one of the greatest lessons of one's life is something else.

Toby and I had gone to India to do some research on Power Places® there, including that greatest of monuments to immortal love, the Taj Mahal. My stepdaughter Rebecca, who was twenty-two at the time, was asked to change Barnaby's water and feed him in my absence. One morning she woke up, and there he was in the bottom of his cage … a stiff, cold, dead cockatiel. Unbeknownst to me at the time, she had called our hotel and spoken to her dad, completely freaked that I'd think she'd killed Barnaby off, or worse, Barnaby died because of her neglect. She swore that she'd been giving the bird water and food.

The next morning, Toby and I were sitting in what has got to be one of the most stunningly beautiful sites in the entire world. The Taj Mahal at sunrise. We'd been sitting, staring at the absolute exquisite magnificence in front of us. We were off to the side of the extensive compound, and no one was around. The depression that had been gripping me for so many months was gently melting a bit in the moment. This beautiful monument to love was in front of me; my beloved husband at my side; our ankles and legs touching; holding hands as we sat on a ledge. The dew in the air and the scent of far-off cooking fires stilled time for me.

All was silent. For the first time in over a year, I could sense being alive. I was at peace. Looking straight ahead, Toby whispered, "Barnaby died." Everything froze, I felt nothing, my breathing stopped, and my heart speed up. "How? When?" I asked. Toby held me, I cried ... although just a little. I had Toby call Rebecca to tell her to do absolutely nothing with the cage, just leave Barnaby's house alone. She had already taken the body to the vet so there was nothing I could do about that. I barely thought about Barnaby the rest of the trip, surprising seeing as how many years I'd had him and how close I was to him.

In looking back, I see that due to my depression and then shock, I was unable to register and express my emotion in that moment about Barnaby dying. We returned home and I purposefully took almost a week before going downstairs to where Rebecca had left his cage. There it was, on the floor by the downstairs door, covered over by the old light blue sheet that I used as his house cover at night. I walked up to within five feet of his cage and just stared at it. Couldn't walk up closer. After a few minutes of staring and letting things sink in, I turned on my heel and quickly walked away. There was a tiny tightening in my chest, which I quickly squelched. Weeks went by. It was easy not to go downstairs, as just Toby's office and Rebecca's rooms were there.

In that time, during meditation and reflection, I decided to have a ceremony, a memorial of sorts, in Barnaby's name. There could not be a burial because I had no body, but I could have a goodbye ceremony. A ceremony is one way to mark an ending. If you make a ceremony or have a ritual such as a memorial, then at least one person is a witness to that event, to the life passage, or to the end of something. Closure is the cliché word we use.

What became undeniable in the weeks that went by was that I was resigned with the thought that I had killed Barnaby. That is not a rational thought, but remember, these were not rational times for me. I had killed Barnaby, plain and simple. I had ignored him, withdrawn love, wasn't there, took him for granted, left him for days in a corner where he'd have no interaction with anything else alive. I went from thinking I'd killed him to thinking he died from neglect ... same thing, guilty as charged. Cockatiels live for a long time, I had been told, up to fifteen years, but he was only ten.

I started looking at my treatment of Barnaby and how I was treating the humans in my life the same way. In the weeks symbolized by Barnaby's covered cage, I went from that black hole of depression and not feeling, to guilt and shame. Not fun emotions, but at least I was feeling *something*. This was a step up the ladder from the "hole."

I told myself I had to pick a date for Barnaby's "memorial." I needed to move on from this hysterical morass in which I was cycling. I wanted to celebrate, to witness that this little bird had brought so much to my life. This little creature could make me smile and be happy just to look at him. From the first moment, he went directly to a special corner in my heart. Now it was time to leave the grief. It was time to celebrate what he brought to my life or rather what his presence had brought out in me when he was alive.

I picked the next Sunday and gave myself a week. Every day, I frequently thought about that day coming up, Barnaby's memorial day. You know how your mind drifts off to a future event that is important to you, and you don't know how it will go? I did not know what I was going to do; I made no plans. I just figured I'd know what to do when the day came.

Sunday came and it was interesting to see how relieved I felt. My senses were more acute that morning than they had been for over a year. Inside, I felt tiny glimmerings of my old self. I decided that this little salutation to Barnaby would take place upstairs in our Tower Room. This was a nine by twelve enclosed glass room, making up the third floor of our home situated on a hill a thousand feet up from the ocean. The Tower Room looked over the treetops to a huge expanse of the Pacific, and one could see up the coast for over twenty miles on a clear day. The hawks and buzzards would circle in front of the house following the currents of wind. The septuagenarian eucalyptus trees, standing over five stories high, proudly and strongly stretched out their massive canopies, providing a dramatic background behind.

No doubt about it, this was the perfect place to celebrate a life form that had made an impact on earth. This place, this Tower Room, between earth, sky, nature, and the ocean, seemed fitting.

At 2 p.m. I started gathering up the things I wanted to have present at this memorial. How do I remember 2 p.m.? It was like an alarm clock went off inside me at 2 p.m. I went to look for items that were special to bring to the remembrance. Facing west and the Pacific, I laid an antique weaving from the Quechua people in Chinchero, Peru, on the leather ottoman in front of the bay windows that were wide open. This antique weaving is full of many esoteric symbols from the ancient Andean culture and religion. This cloth had been with me to many of the ancient Incan temples throughout Peru. I got out my hand-carved pipe from Palenque, Mexico. On one side is carved an owl and on the other, a bat, symbols of the Underworld.

In the Native American tradition, I wanted to send prayers by way of smoke. Burning sage serves the purpose of "cleaning out" a space, and sweetgrass attracts good energy. An alabaster hand-carved small bowl from the West Bank in Egypt with some sand at the bottom held the tablet of charcoal that would burn the Mayan cobal incense from the Yucatan. In the center of this altar, I would place Barnaby's chest down feathers from the bottom of his cage that I had finally cleaned out the day before. So here I sat upstairs, preparing the space, making an altar of sorts.

Suddenly, from outside down below, I heard Rebecca yelling, "Teri, Teri, come outside, a bird just fell out of the sky and dropped down on the driveway, and I think it's dead!" I rushed outside and sure enough, there was a huge gray dove with small specks of white around its beak ... dead as a doorknob. I just stared at it for the longest time. Then, surprisingly and quite casually as I recall, I thought to take the pigeon upstairs. This dove would be Barnaby's surrogate body. Now I could have an official funeral ... I had a body!

I couldn't pick up the dove at first, as it was too creepy to touch something dead that was still warm and soft. By the time I got the courage to pick it up, the sun was just starting to set. I took the dead dove upstairs, wrapped in a cloth. Ever so gently, I laid it on the Peruvian weaving.

It was a beautiful picture, if I say so myself. I just stared at that bird, aware of the silence all around. In the space of the day, just after sunset and just before complete darkness, there is usually a special silence and energy that can be experienced if we take the time and just pause. I remember the stillness well, no breeze at all because as I lit the sage and sweetgrass, the smoke went straight up.

I waved the braid of sage and sweetgrass over the bird and the altar. I let the smoke go over my head, rubbed my hands over it, and let it float over the front of my body as I knelt in front of the ottoman where the altar was. I started to speak softly, expressing why I was there. Before I knew it, I was saying out loud, "Barnaby, I am sorry I ignored you and cut you out of my life." And with those words, a sob from the deepest part of my heart came boiling and bubbling up and out of my entire body, and I just wept and wept and wept.

I cried because I really missed this little creature who made me feel so welcome in the world. I cried because I felt guilty and ashamed at my neglect—of him, and the people I loved. I cried because of all the times in my life that I had neglected or rejected. I cried because I was miserable. I cried because I missed God. I cried for all the missed opportunities in my life. I cried because I never had to explain anything to Barnaby when I was alive; we just could be together. I did not take advantage of that. The whole time, the glassy eye of the dead dove just stared at me. I really missed Barnaby!

I wouldn't say he was a person to me as some people feel about their pets. Honestly, to this day, I wouldn't say I am a pet person. I would say I loved him. People joke about a dog heaven or cat heaven. Well, is it so silly to think that there is a bird heaven? If not heaven, then a place where bird consciousness goes to, or do all things that are alive go to the same place when they are no longer alive in the earth realm? Makes sense, based on my experience when Grandma Rosie died.

In the middle of his funeral, I started calling Barnaby in my thoughts. I wished he could come around one more time so I could say goodbye. In the whole world in this silent moment, there was only me, the altar, the dead bird lying in front of me with its unblinking eye fixed right on me, the far-off ocean, the quiet, still air, and a sense of expansiveness all around. The far-off distant city lights sparkled below the deepening dark sky about an hour past sunset.

Suddenly, the wind started blowing, rattling and slamming the open windows like crazy. I'll only report what happened next. I distinctly heard Barnaby's chirps. It was so loud, as if he was at my earlobe. The wind blew and I could feel Barnaby's wingtips ever so gently swishing past first one cheek then the other. It was as if he was flying in front of me in big swoops. Then all of a sudden—silence. It was gone. I was so happy.

Comments: Rebecca found the dead Barnaby. She also found the dead dove. The dove dropped out of the sky the afternoon of the designated memorial service right onto our driveway: plop. A huge sudden wind, out of nowhere, coming from the west— unusual, it usually came from the north. All I know is I was healed of the guilt, felt forgiven, and was at peace. I had closure with Barnaby after that day. Interestingly, I was up out of the "dark hole."

A few weeks later, I was running a tour to Stonehenge, Avebury, and other Power Places® in England. Buying postcards, I saw one with a painting of a cat, which for some reason caught my eye. (I am definitely not a cat person.) The painting was of a black cat with four white socks, a white throat and chin, and gorgeous velvety fur. It sat regally up on a windowsill. Elegantly propped up on its forelegs, its head was turned to the artist with a serene look to its sweet face and clear eyes. Not giving much thought to it, I bought the postcard. It ended up in my closet stationery box stashed with old photos, postcards, and bits of stationery from our worldly travels.

Over the years, I'd go to the box and use the postcards purchased in my travels as stationery. Once in a while, I'd run across this postcard with the cat on a windowsill. I'd look at it and wonder why I had even bought it and why I continued to keep it as I'm not a cat fan. Then I'd put it back in the box. That postcard sat in the box for years, easily forgotten.

In 1995, Toby and I decided it was time to start planning for future retirement. He thought it would fit the bill to buy a little house in the tropics that we could live in perhaps half a year when we retire, and that we could enjoy now a few weeks out of the year and rent it out as a private Power Place® the rest of the year. Holding the healing energy of Bali, and Gili Meno Beach right off its coast as our ideal, we found a place in St. Croix, the U.S. Virgin Islands.

It was hell and back to make that place, built in the fifties, livable. But that's another story. One night very late, shortly after our first official overnight in the house when the first phase of the major reconstruction was finally finished, I heard a loud, pathetic, high-pitched pseudo-meowing right outside the living room sliding door. There sat a tiny little ball of yucky fur. The fur mass was wailing and crying.

Now here was the dilemma. We were here for a couple of weeks only, new to the island, still getting organized, and had not arranged for a housesitter for when we left. Most important, neither of us are cat people. After what seemed like a long time, the wailing and meowing ceased, I looked, and the kitty was gone. I breathed a sigh of relief that I did not have to make any decisions about that matted furball. I could stop feeling guilty for not feeding it. The kitten was quickly forgotten.

Late the next night, the high-pitched meowing and wailing

began emanating again at the same sliding glass door, from that same tiny mass of fur with a very skinny frame underneath. I must say, it was a mass of fur with huge, protruding, haunted wild eyes. I became more anxious as the minutes went by, and it looked like the kitten wasn't going away this time. It must be lost from its mother and was living wild in the forested ravine right next to the house, too young and too inexperienced to be a "mouser." The high-pitched howling got louder and louder and more persistent. It was hard to believe that this minute little ball of fur could be making that much racket.

I moved across the room to the screen door to get a closer look. No doubt about it, this ball of fur was starving. I went into action and grabbed a little half-and-half cream and mixed it with a little tuna, figuring high fat and protein content would fill its belly. As soon as I opened the door, it ran away. Setting down the little bowl outside on the walkway a few feet from the door, I walked back in the house and hid in the shadows. A few short moments later, the kitty cautiously appeared and looked around as it threw caution to the wind, went straight for the bowl, and bolted down the food. When it was finished, it looked quickly from left to right, then slinked back in the dark into the thick brush and trees of the ravine. The next night, it returned, gave a few miserable howls, and I was there with food. It was definitely a wild thing and had not been around humans. Only out of desperation when it was starving did it come to the house.

The morning after that, it appeared on the lawn and just sat down, about twenty feet from the door, a little black spot on the lush green lawn. As I brought the food out (it was not cat food, as I hadn't 100 percent broken down yet to buy some), it ditched back into the canopy of the forest. I set the bowl down and waited patiently. No furball. Going back into the house, I watched as it came out when the coast was clear and delicately ate in a confident manner. It was no longer starving. Looking at its cute little head sunk into the small, but to her gigantic, bowl, I felt my heart warm and commented to myself, "Looks like you've got yourself a kitty, great, just what you don't want." The saving grace I thought to myself is that cats, unlike dogs, don't bug you. They are around, you pet them, then they leave, and you both can go back to doing your own thing.

The next few days, it trained me in the ritual of delivering her food. I'd leave it at a respectable distance, and she'd gingerly approach and eat it. Eventually, it allowed me to stay as I left the food at the designated area and sat in ever-closer distances as the days went by. I wanted to get close to touch this little creature that now was making its presence known in my heart. One day, I was only six feet away after setting the bowl down. I waited. Its little head popped out from the bushes after a couple of minutes, and I could sense her surprise to see me so close to the reward. It waited and looked at me; I waited and looked at it. It went in and out of the bush a couple of times, cautiously approaching the bowl and then darting back into the ravine. I sat calm and patient. Eventually, hunger won out as it dashed out, watching me out of the corner of its eye the entire time, gulping down the food. I did not move a muscle. The second day, I repeated the procedure, only I sat three feet away, not moving a muscle. The third day, I held the bowl in my hand. It came.

The fourth day, I sat there, bowl in hand, making little kitten meowing noises and speaking softly. She (after being so close

I could tell there were no testicles) came up and ate. I slowly put my other hand out to touch her, instinctively curling in my fingers, thumb on my third finger like when I'd pick up Barnaby from his cage. Contact! I did not force it, and she did not relax into it. She was trembling but she let me touch. This kitty was such a "cutie pie" and so sweet. If we named her, of course it would be official, and so there it was. "Cutie Pie" she became. She started coming when I called in kitten noises. Feeding her twice a day, she lost all her skinniness. She was a wild outdoor kitty and lived in the rainforest ravine a few yards away, which was fine with us.

We left a week later. Returning to the island three months later, while taking the drive to the house, I wondered if she would be around. Would she remember me? Would she even be around? Three months is a long time, and she was a baby, and I had been gone for the majority of her life.

We pulled off the street into the long driveway. Unbelievable, if she wasn't sitting right there immediately to the side at the entrance. I was very happy, and my heart registered a surprise love and deep connection for this Cutie Pie.

Something happened in the next two weeks that I will put down and record but make no comment or evaluation. I'd hear Barnaby's signature welcome chirp in my head when Cutie Pie would come out of the bushes or around the corner of the house. Now, since Barnaby died, I'd heard his sound every once in a blue moon over the years, but certainly not in recent years. It was exactly what I would hear as I pulled into the driveway after work: his signature greeting. It was different from his other sounds, and he used it only as a welcome if he hadn't seen me.

The first time I heard his chirp after so long, I welcomed the memory but I didn't think more of it. When it kept happening around Cutie Pie's entrance, it got my attention. I noticed more than once that when I'd see Cutie Pie for the first time that day, automatically without thinking, I'd say BarNaby—with the emphasis on the second syllable, the inflection of my voice going up the way I would sing-song Barnaby's name. Oops, I meant "Hello Cutie Pie." A beloved bird—an unsolicited for kitty.

I now really loved Cutie Pie and felt a return of her kitty energy, at least to the hand that fed her. It's been five years now and Barnaby's name never slips from my lips when I see her. Rare is Barnaby's welcome signature sound in my head.

We made the decision to permanently move to St. Croix. We accomplished the hugely distasteful task of packing up in Laguna Beach. In the torture of packing, I went through the closet, eventually reaching the box of postcards and stationery from my travels. Rifling through the box, I asked myself if I was really going to schlep this to the new place. Uncovering the kitty post-card, I stopped and stared, stunned. There was the painting of the gorgeous velvety black cat with the four white socks, white throat and chin, and huge gorgeous eyes sitting in the windowsill. Cutie Pie was the cat in the postcard.

Lifewalkers: Witnesses to the Beginning

I worked for a while as a nurse in the labor and delivery unit. Of all my medical positions, this one provided the happiest moments. Lucky Lifewalkers. We are witnesses to the arrival of a human emerging from the watery realm of the womb. A tiny carbon unit pushed through the cervical opening, or plucked from the womb, inhaling its first breath. It's official; there is a new life amongst our midst on the planet. From nurses, paramedics, midwives, and New York taxi drivers, to efficient but hardened ER Docs who have seen everything, being the first to touch and hold a new human, fresh from the primordial womb, can be a stunning phenomenon, filling one with wonderment. A "peak experience." If not too jaded, for most it is a gift, awe-inspiring. One is energetically connected with that newborn.

Those present may look around at each other, instinctively knowing they have been a witness to something profound, an addition to humanity. It is true, they could be witnesses to an unfortunate soul who is headed for only pain, misery, and the entire gamut of potential tragedy available to the human experience. If asked, each witness probably would have opinions based on their perspective and past experiences as to exactly what they are a witness to. However, make no mistake, they have been a witness.

Unequivocally, one person always present as a witness is the woman who has given birth. She was there from the beginning when that carbon unit came into existence.* The woman whose uterus has cradled the fetus is the ultimate "Lifewalker." She nurtured this creation in her holy cave usually for around nine months.

Contractions signal the process has begun. The carbon unit has started its journey toward the dense world and limitations of physical form outside the womb. During labor, all factors matter, impacting the infant's subtle life energies. The mother's mood and attitude about the new life she's about to bring forth, the father's presence or lack thereof, support from others, and the environment. The newborn emerges from its protected holy cave via the "funnel of destiny," the cervix and vagina. Out of its water world into a world where gravity rules but the element of air reigns supreme.

The mother or other primary caretaker(s) feeds, rocks, cradles, provides warmth, protection, loving care, and mentoring as the newborn grows stronger, expanding and developing its physical, mental, and emotional traits. Science and experience have proven the most important ingredient is l-o-v-e. Love is the intangible "sealant" binding all the supportive intentions, care, and nurturing, providing a maximum potential with a good shot at fulfilling its destiny once it separates from the family.

*The question as to when a human being "begins" its existence is beyond the purview of this book. I will leave that matter of discussion to scientists, philosophers, religious institutions, and to Jane Doe/GQ Public.

If the coconut never separates from the coconut tree, it can never become its own tree. That is its destiny; that is what it was meant to be. That is the natural order.

" WELCOME PRECIOUS ONE"

Welcome, welcome, oh most precious One.

The entire earth sends love and we do hope you stay.

To laugh, to twirl, to swim, and to play,

To explore, to learn, and to share our days.

Welcome dearest (insert name of child here), you are so loved,

You are special, you are cherished,

You are a great treasure to us all.

A greeting to be spoken in a "sing-song" way
while attending a birth or seeing a newborn for the first time

Life, Death, and Before: Knights in Battle

Growing up, I always had a great fear of my father dying. I was absolutely convinced that when he died, so would I, literally. I would also die. It's not that I love him more than my beloved mother. Her death will be a real watershed in my life; however, I didn't think that would cause me to die. As a child, I knew I would die when Dad did, as sure as I knew I couldn't stand playing with dolls.

The answer to the mystery of why I felt that way revealed itself unceremoniously one day when Toby and I were in Southern France. We were researching the Knights Templar and legends about the Holy Grail for our travel company in the mid-nineties. We were in the medieval town of Albi. The charm and antiquity of the places and the manner of the shopkeepers and townspeople made it easy to be immersed in the feeling of what life must have been like there centuries ago.

That night lying next to Toby while drifting off to sleep, I had a half-vision or "flash," as I call it. It occurred during that time we all experience as the "twilight zone." Those moments when we are just starting to drift off to sleep but are aware.

It was a gray day as I now saw myself standing on a huge open plain. I was a man in my early twenties, dressed in a suit of armor. I was charged on adrenaline ("pumped up" is the manly term, I guess), extremely alert, all my senses acutely tuned as they never had been before. I was on a battlefield in the middle of a battle.

Fascinated from my twilight zone state, I surveyed the scene. Then the sound came, a muffled cacophony of metal clashing, blood spewing, the thud of bodies falling, and horses screaming and crashing into each other. Simultaneously, there wasn't any sound except my breathing. I know, this makes no sense.

I did not have a helmet on, but some sort of close-fitting metal sheet head covering. A man in his late fifties was in front of me, like a wall. I eyed him with a cold, hard, and distinctly pure hatred. The land of my people land had been seized, and it was my responsibility to retrieve ownership at all costs. In the battle between the clans/families and their allies, my youth and battle experience were a distinct advantage.

The despised man in front of me was the head of the other clan. In him was everything I wanted to eliminate, to exterminate, to crush the breath out of. Fueled by a mighty fire of righteousness, I went for his throat with all of my youthful prowess and strength. We fell to the ground, I on top of him, my hands around his neck and throat.

I watched his face as I deliberately squeezed the life out of him. I couldn't stop myself. I did not want to stop. My hands kept on squeezing and squeezing. As I was squeezing, it was as if time stopped. I could see the life slowly draining out until the cup was empty. There was no breath. A strange stillness lay in my hands.

As the young warrior, I had absolutely no emotional response to what just happened. A sense of justice and victory started to skate across the higher centers of my cerebral cortex. Then something happened that prevented the mental victory dance to be completed. I mentally made a note, before I physically felt, a huge spear ripping through my back, crashing through major organs, and severing my spine.

At the same time, I (me now) looked at the lifeless face below me. It was the face of my dad in this life now! He was the old warrior I had just killed on the battlefield.

This young warrior fell on top of the old man from the other family. I was dead as a dodo bird in the blink of an eye. The spear was sticking straight up like a huge toothpick in a smoked oyster. I, as myself now, saw who had "run me through," who had snuffed me out from behind. The son of the old man warrior had shifted the fortunes of the clans by running me through moments after I, as the young warrior, had played God with his father.

This "son" turned out to be my present-day brother! As myself, a bomb exploded in my head, and a million questions arose simultaneously. No wonder I am afraid of dying when my dad dies — because at one time I did die when he died!

Is there such a thing as past lives? Did my brain make up all of these biological and neurochemical shenanigans to deal with some buried psychological terrors I was harboring? During my half-awake state, was this an attempt to make order in some part of my psyche that can't imagine the pain of my dying Daddy? I still don't know for sure.

Thereafter, my "unasked for" and "not looked for" experience in Albi permanently settled my angst about my father dying. My beloved dad will someday die as everyone eventually does. There will be great pain and suffering and a sense of loss for the rest of my life, but I literally don't have to die about it. I will still go on living.

Volumes have been written about reincarnation. Is it a fact somehow hidden in our DNA, cascading brain neurochemical synaptic firings, fantasy, delusion, or ?? It's interesting that proof has been offered in many well-documented cases around the world.

Being in Albi, walking through the thirteenth century cobblestone alleyways and exploring the medieval fortress, had somehow triggered memories of another life. Toby and I had experienced medieval towns in Europe many times before. Why this town, why now? Someday I would love to return to Albi. Is it possible that there had been a battle here between two clans, following the same storyline of my "twilight zone" remembrance? That would indeed be fun to find out.

Mammy and Her Laddy

In August of 1995, I was on my first vacation alone. It had been a non-stop, busy month of leading groups in Egypt. I needed some breathing space. A visit to magical Ireland without an agenda or mandatory schedule fit the bill perfectly. Toby and I had first visited Ireland a few years back. Throughout that trip, I was moved by an unexplainable deep connection to this mystical island. I had vowed to return on a regular basis to the Ol' Sod that felt exactly like home. Coincidentally, a dear friend and colleague would be in Ireland at the same time to visit his dying mother. His dear "Mammy" was suffering from cancer and apparently had not very long to live.

Philip had moved fifteen years ago to the U.S. from Ireland to attend medical school at Harvard. Now he was a highly respected neurologist with a thriving private practice in a "toney" Southern California beach town. He was rapidly making a national name for himself as a leading expert on chronic headaches, a debilitating medical problem for over thirty-eight million people in the U.S. As a Family Medicine Nurse Practitioner, I managed his "Headache Institute," taking the patients through the multifaceted treatment plan he designed for them.

We were both beginning our journeys in Dublin. He to visit family members, I to return to the ancient Power Places® of Newgrange and Knowth, potent mystical sites Toby and I experienced on our initial trip. Philip and I would drive from Dublin to his boyhood home in historical Listowel to spend a couple of days with his mammy and youngest sister. Home to many world-famous authors and poets, Listowel is located in the wild west end of Ireland in northern County Kerry.

While working together, Philip had regaled me with stories of growing up in this tiny, deeply Catholic traditional Irish village. He was mesmerizing when delivering those tales, a natural-born storyteller. He also had this beautiful tenor voice, which came in handy to help cover expenses when he was in medical school. He reminded me of what a Seanchaí in ancient Ireland must have been like. The Seanchaí (shan-a-key) were traditional Irish storytellers and singers of ballads. For millennia, they kept the Celtic history, culture, myths, and folklore alive. They would travel from village to village, entrancing the local populace with legendary tales and the singing of melodic ballads.

Prior to the formation of the EU, Ireland had been considered one of the poorer areas by many other countries of Europe. A fiery and majestically proud people, the Celts had a millennia-old and magnificent history. They were an ancient civilization whose engineers built spectacular earthworks and awe-inspiring gigantic ceremonial mounds. However, they never recovered from the almost-genocidal tactics deployed by the English in the 1840s during the potato famine.

Growing up very poor, Philip lived with his parents and ten siblings in a two-story home with one bathroom and two bedrooms. At bedtime, the children all packed into the tiny bedrooms, two beds in each. While sleeping, one was lucky to have a back right up to your face instead of someone's feet. With the bedrooms upstairs, only one person at a time could navigate the narrow steps leading from the tiny upstairs landing down to the living room and kitchen.

I drove as we traversed the narrow winding roads in the countryside between Dublin in the east to Listowel in the west. We didn't engage in our usual lively banter considering the seriousness of the trip. After driving all day, we arrived at his childhood home in the dark of evening.

Philip was quiet as we walked from the low-lit street, up the long, thin sidewalk, to the house. The silence was absolute until, to the left behind the high wall of trees and bushes that marked the property's boundary on one side, I could hear an occasional cough. I wondered to myself who would be over there in the dark. Later, I found out that the coughing sounds originated from a nearby herd of cows.

Walking into the cheerful living room, we were greeted by his darling kid sister Jean. It was immediately apparent that Jean adored her big brother. She couldn't do too much for him. They decided to wait until morning to visit with their mammy, as it was late. Besides, everyone was spent, understandably so.

The next morning, Jean and Philip entered the small downstairs bedroom that had been built for Mammy a few years before. Slowly, Philip walked up to the bed and greeted his mammy in a way that can only be done when you see your beloved mother dying in front of you. I waited outside in the narrow hall. From the doorway, I could see his dear "Mammy" wearing an apparently freshly ironed cotton nightgown and lying on a comfortable-looking bed made up with what looked like fresh linen. Her hair had been smoothly brushed. It was obvious that Jean was pouring TLC into the smallest little tasks. My heart ached for these three. Standing there, Philip's baby sister spoke to them in a soft and soothing voice. It was evident his dear mammy was cogent one moment, forgetful and confused the next.

After a while, Philip and his sister left the room. I walked in quietly and sat down on the floor right next to the low bed. Introducing myself, and who I was to Philip, I asked her if she would mind sharing with me any memories that particularly stood out for her of Philip. This mother of eleven paused for a long time. Looking over my head, I imagined her reviewing her life for specific memories of her second-to-youngest child.

Instead, she replied, "There were so many, it's hard to remember." She meant so many children. There was a long pause as she closed her eyes and gave a sigh. I sat there, wishing I could see what she was remembering. She lay there, I sat there, both with our own thoughts. The house was deeply silent too. After a while, I took her hand, squeezed it, softly said, "I'll be back later," and tiptoed out of the room.

The house was peaceful and quiet the next morning as I returned alone and again sat on the floor, leaning on the bed in order to get as close as I could. The sun cast a beautiful, soft light through the sheer curtains. I would not let her rest this time. On looking back, this took a lot of audacity on my part. Here was I, a perfect stranger, wishing her to reveal an intimate memory. However, I was on an unasked-for-mission for Philip, who I not only cared deeply for but always felt protective towards for some unexplainable reason. Why? I really wanted to be able to relay even just snippets of motherly remembrances to him from long ago. Perhaps as a baby, or as a sweet child growing up with ten other siblings in the backward countryside of County Kerry in the fifties and sixties. I wanted to tell him what she told me and what she could never tell him directly. How much she loved her caring and extremely successful, brilliant Harvard Medical School Chief Resident, board-certified neurologist psychiatrist son, who had achieved the impossible. Coming out of this small village, he now had everything in the world: a beautiful, intelligent wife who was crazy about him; two children whom he lived and breathed by; a brilliant career in medicine with a successful practice in a well-to-do upscale city in Southern California; a palatial home in an exclusive gated community in the hills above the Pacific Ocean; and all the material trappings one could hope for.

He had everything, except for one thing. The ultimate human experience of the exquisite sweetness of hearing the sound of his dear Mammy's voice in his ear, whispering, "I love ya, laddy."

I wanted him to experience with his mom the nurturing, all-enveloping connection that happens with the verbal exchange of the ultimate "L" word, love. I am most fortunate to have experienced that frequently with my beloved mom my entire life, as a matter of course. Knowing how much my mother loves me is one thing. Growing up with her expressing this complete, unconditional love with words and the clear expression of this unconditional love with deeds in umpteenth ways, even with seven other children, had been a huge comfort and security in my formative years.

I wanted to be the bearer of the gift of the "L" word and phrase from Philip's mammy to him. I knew far better than he what a comfort it would bring to his heart and soul. The completion of some circle that he had always been dancing with his mammy, and his life in general. A circle that I could only guess at. An experience for Philip that might provide a key to an internal puzzle. A key that could bring a feeling of great comfort at the back of his heart where only his children had been allowed to enter.

One has to understand the Irish culture in regard to expressing or emulating the emotion of love to one another. They don't. On the other hand, they are some of the most deeply loving and emotional people in the world. They generally just cannot express love or speak about it out loud, except through their poetry or music. They have backhanded ways for expressing love. Any sign of affection or love is most often uttered in the guise of a joke, caustic remark, or sarcastic phrase.

Mammy's voice was weak and frequently drifted off to an almost inaudible whisper. "There were so many, it is hard to separate them, remembering them." So she was trying to remember. As I was not around when her children were growing up, I could not jog the old gal's memory with "Well, remember when we all ..." or "...wasn't that great craic (the Irish term for fun) when he ..."

I asked, "What would you say about Philip?" She replied, "He is so generous and kind to his sister and me. He's always been such a good lad." (I knew Philip had been financially providing for them for years, so she had to be speaking specifically about him.)

Her light blue eyes had a faraway look. Her voice faded; she closed her eyes. I asked her what was her favorite music. In what can only be described as a "very sweet young" voice, she replied, "Paddy singing," and proceeded to tell me the name of the song which I can't recall now. I replied, "Let's play Paddy." There was a little table against the wall with a cassette player and a couple of tapes on it. I put in the Paddy Reilly tape with the song she mentioned ready to play and left the room bringing Philip back with me. "Philip," I said, "your mammy's favorite," pointing to the player and meaning the song that was ready to play. I fluffed her pillow and propped up her head to make her more comfortable as she lay facing the table across the tiny room.

Paddy's haunting voice began, and Philip turned to look at the cassette player. I, too, looked at the cassette player and ended up standing between Philip and his mammy. As Paddy unfolded his exquisitely sweet soaring tenor, it seemed as if the whole world came to a standstill. The beautiful a cappella notes dreamily drifted out over the landscape. I imagined them painting her memories on the lush green hills of the countryside where she'd lived her life.

It was palpable, this exquisite moment. Time stopped. Her favorite Irish tenor singing, Mammy lying in bed dying, her mind going to those places and events where only dying people's minds go, her second-to-youngest having the bittersweet torture of hearing Mammy's "favorite" song with her as she lay dying.

Instinctively, I took Mammy's left hand in my right hand, and Philip's right hand in my left. While I could have put their hands together and left the room, I didn't think of that at the time. The three of us formed a chain of living flesh brought together with this soaring sound that formed a conduit to a timeless place where it was impossible not to deeply connect with each other.

The song ended; the cassette clicked off. The silence was profound. The flowers on the wallpaper were larger, brighter, almost third-dimensional. Philip quietly walked out without a word. Mammy quietly rolled over to her right side facing the wall, without a word. I stood there for a moment in the middle of this tiny bedroom, knowing I had just been a part of a profound experience. Philip and I drove away the next morning. That was the last time he saw his mammy.

Approximately six weeks later, Toby and I were in Switzerland on a hiking trip before going onward to Egypt to conduct a tour. One morning, driving down the hill on our way to a local hot springs and spa, I slammed on the brakes, turned to Toby, and said, "I think Philip's mother just died." I cried silently for my dear friend Philip who never did hear those exquisite "L" words from Mammy, and now never would. I called him when we got to Egypt. He'd just returned from the funeral in Ireland.

To Be or Not to Be

At approximately 11:30 a.m. on Thursday, November 16, 2000, Hurricane Lenny began shouting his landfall presence in St. Croix. At 3:30 p.m., I journaled about it. This was our first "hurricane experience." It took me a moment to remember what day of the week it was. A direct hit from a Category 4 hurricane, with sustained winds of 155 mph, has that effect.

Hurricane Lenny was spinning clockwise, moving in the opposite direction for hurricanes north of the equator. "Wrong Way Lenny," as the National Hurricane Center meteorologists started calling it, was spinning West-East, a never-before-seen phenomenon in the 129 years that the U.S. had been keeping track of hurricanes.

Like all hurricanes, "Lenny" was made up of "rain bands" on the outside, and in the middle, an "eye wall" containing the strongest winds and rains, and at the center, the "eye." On any one day, an average hurricane releases as much energy as half a million atomic bombs.

The elements of water (the ocean) and air make up hurricanes. Three things need to occur simultaneously to create such a phenomenon: warm ocean water at least 79 degrees, damp air, and a sustained wind per minute of minimum 74 mph. Once these factors combine for a consistent period of time, a hurricane forms as the earth continues its rotational pull on it.

"Wrong Way Lenny" had begun its relentless march across the Caribbean three days earlier. We had executed Toby's detailed hurricane "prep" checklist earlier in the week. This included putting up all the important metal hurricane shutters and securing thick stainless steel cables, anchored by 3 foot cement pillars sunk in the lawn, over the roof. The full fury of this circular, spiraling vehicle was now at our door.

I'll never understand my urge to experience this chaotic maelstrom of Mother Nature for myself. However, "Wrong Way Lenny" was like a magnet. I just had to step outside, even for just a couple of minutes. I had to know what it felt like. Knowing full well that Toby would have a fit if he knew what I was thinking, understandably so. I didn't say a word beforehand. I didn't change my clothes, keeping on my sleeveless T-shirt, shorts, and flip-flops. I paused at the front door, yelling over my shoulder, "Honey, I'll be right back!" slamming the door shut before I could hear any response.

The front door faced away from Lenny's fury, which was coming straight from the west. Later, I figured I must have gone out as the "eye wall," with its strongest winds and rains, was passing through. I turned right, staying close to the front of the house, concentrating on carefully walking the seventy feet to the end of the front of the house, and turned right again.

People mention "the roar of the hurricane." In that moment, that phrase seemed an understatement. I was hit by a wall of what I can only describe as a "primordial howling." Even though it was daytime, the sunlight could barely filter through the veil of exploding rain. Rain was spewing upside down; rain was blowing horizontally. The wind was barreling in simultaneously from all directions. Meeting themselves, the wind's atoms detonated in a loud roar. The air was dense and thick with salt from the sea. This strange air was almost too heavy to breath in.

Continuing to inch my way toward the ocean, I was stunned at the sight barely visible through the salty haze. Our usual smooth-as-glass sparkling turquoise Caribbean Sea had transformed into an alchemical frothing giant cauldron. Humongous twenty- to twenty-five-foot-tall waves, seething, and with no space in between, were breaking less than a hundred feet out from our home. The fifteen-foot cliff prevented the relentlessly pounding surf from reaching the house, at least for the moment. Tentatively stepping away from the house, I looked at the palm trees, expecting they'd all be horizontal by then. They were bent, with their fronds all bending to the east, pliable, in harmony with the wind movement. The hibiscus and Ginger-Thomas flower bushes were not so lucky. Their demise was evident in the air and on the ground. For what seemed like a long while, I stood there. The howling, the roaring, the threatening waves sounded like heavy gun artillery being fired off a battleship. I have to admit it was electrifying. A world turned upside down, complete and utter chaos and destruction. Nothing was as it should be. I suddenly came to my senses and gingerly made my way back.

Slipping back through the front door, I went looking for Toby. He asked me where I'd been, knowing full well where I had been. I didn't answer. He just looked at me. I knew he'd been worried.

After twenty-one years together, he recognized that when I was on a "mission," nothing or no one could stop me. Since I was three years old, that has been true. Even my saintly mom was unable to dissuade me from climbing rocks, hanging from the jungle gym, or trying to jump down off the swing—no matter how she tried to distract me. If I was determined to experience something, then somehow and in some way, I would. And importantly, do it all by myself, rejecting anyone's support or help.

It was only decades later that I came to regret that misguided staunch independent streak. It would turn out to be a major flaw in my long-term intimate relationships, frequently blocking the very closeness I craved. But that's another story. It was only when my beloved Toby read the first draft of this book that he learned the details of this wild sojourn.

Standing inside the house, I had a huge smile; I was on a natural endorphin high. My lungs were "sparkling," for want of a better term. The rawness of the elemental forces had touched every piece of matter in its environment. Had moved it, energized it, or altered it in some way. Including me.

In nature, sometimes change is deadly, like the calabash gourd from the tree in the front yard. The gourd was twirled, bounced around, and smashed to smithereens. This force touched the underbelly of every blade of grass, and it touched me. A "peak experience," this was an experience of another world.

Nature is a reminder of the basic natural cycles of life. One could say that any hurricane or any intense episode of nature powerfully unfurling reflects the multiple intertwining cycles of life. Creation, destruction, followed by chaos, and then homeostasis, and new life.

We smile; the smile dies. A leaf falls off a tree, dead. However prior to it's disconnecting, it had already died. The wind affects the trajectory of the leaves's descent. The leaf falls and lands on something below it based on wind speed or lack of wind, the weight of the leaf, and the original location of the leaf on the mother tree. Will it lie there and stay put? Or will the wind, an animal, an insect, or a two-legged creature move it from this place? Did it land on dirt, fertile soil, concrete, gravel, in a yard, or on the rainforest floor?

Every second of every day we disconnect, dry out, or die of something within ourselves. The choices we make in those moments, like the wind coming, affects our trajectory, landing point, and eventual recycling.

Whether internal hurricanes, a swirling tornado of life events, or a sudden tropical storm of disappointment, we have a choice every moment of how we will consciously respond. How we will act or react based on that moment in front of us. It is *never really* about the other person or about the situation. It is about "ourselves" internally. That is all that matters. That of taking full responsibility for our thoughts and our actions. The first time I really experienced this to be true, I hated that notion, it really ticked me off! However, the resultant freedom has been incredible, albeit very uncomfortable at times, I must admit.

Do you choose the path of freedom, and thus with a conscious *"awareness"* make your own way? Or do you take the path of least resistance? Do you continue to be enmeshed in the "same ol', same ol,'" or make excuses strewn with "yes ... but(s)," feeling sorry for yourself?

So what will it be? Will you choose to really "live?" Or will you choose to continue to stay in one of your comfort zones, thus dying a little more every day? To BE or NOT to BE? That is the question.

Our VIPs: We Are Not the Same After They Die

Everyone has a handful of VIPs in their life if they're lucky. VIPs bring a special "something" to your life that no one else has brought. When a VIP dies, things will never quite be the same. It is a milestone when they die; their absence is irreplaceable.

Here I am, a few new white hairs away from turning fifty, and Grandma Rosie is my first VIP to die.* Throughout millennia, volumes have been written and sung about the emotional, spiritual, and psychic pain when someone we love passes. From our travels around the world, it is clear how we in the West live in fear of getting old and aging. We go to inordinate attempts to avoid even facing the question of our mortality, and drive ourselves mad trying to avoid it.

Eastern philosophy sees endings, death, and change as only parts of a huge cycle known as life or existence. Realizing and, importantly, accepting that death, change/rebirth, and life just *are* would be a huge step in overcoming and moving through this

*When I wrote this chapter years ago, Grandma Rosie was my only VIP who had passed. Since then, my beloved Toby and my parents also have passed.

fear we have of death.

Death in some ways is an all-pervasive part of our daily lives. We are so fearful and uncomfortable with it that we ignore it, deny it, disguise it, camouflage it, repress it, surgically remove it, run away from it, misname it, and deliberately refuse to recognize it.

In going around, everything comes around, including new life. From a certain perspective, death is around every minute of one's existence. We smile and then we don't. The smile dies. We blink and see the bird flying against the sky. It soars out of our vision, another death. The scene no longer exists in our reality.

The tragedy is that in trying to avoid death, we avoid truly "living." We want to freeze only the life, the creation part. Perhaps not the creation part because creating implies there is an aspect of chaos. To be precise, we want to freeze the ordered, structured part of life, the dependable part that gives us some comfort or joy.

I want to "freeze" the moment Toby gave me that bouquet of roses for my forty-ninth birthday. That moment he looked right at me, his eyes sparkling with all the love he has for me, even after all these years. Yes, I want to freeze that moment.

A wave begins to take shape way out in the ocean. Currents, air temperature, water temperature, salt content, storms, and the ocean floor all contribute to making this wave. It begins to crest rapidly, whitewater forms, it comes down, and in a flash, meets itself on the shore, spent of dynamic energy.

We never know how long the beloved VIPs will be in our oceans. Too often we take life for granted, including what we do or do not say. The following are suggested guidelines for communications with our VIPs and others we love. And actually, to anyone we have contact with.

Be kind. Be considerate. Be respectful. Be polite. Speak and act with good manners. If in the presence of an elder, don't talk back sassy or be a smart-alec. Be compassionate. Listen with mindfulness.

Don't yell. Don't hit anyone, ever, no matter what.

Don't speak out of anger. Wait, count to ten, and then speak. If still royally ticked off, then count to ten...again.

Before giving your opinion, add a long pause. A longer pause, *please*, if you are not asked for your opinion!

Importantly, tell them you love them. Thank them for being in your life.

Communications from the "OtherSide"

W hen someone close to us dies, we may find ourselves spontaneously talking to them, either out loud or in our heads. And those who have passed most likely will be reaching out to us from the "OtherSide." For a variety of reasons, we don't hear or sense communications returning to us. These episodes of communications from those who have departed, by their very nature, bring in a matter very controversial.

Although anecdotal, this phenomenon of communications from the "OtherSide" has been documented for hundreds of years. What are these phenomena that many have experienced, whether a person admits to them or not? I will leave that to be answered by neuroscientists, philosophers, and spiritual counselors.

Like millions, I have been fortunate to have had experiences and communications from those who are on the OtherSide. In sharing these encounters, and a couple that my mother had with my grandmother, perhaps readers may remember similar events that have happened to them. In my experience, it is in the remembering that a healing at some level is likely to take place. And in that healing, we can realize a closure, or a new level of acceptance.

My large, close, extended Mexican-American family and friends were holding a fiftieth birthday party for my dad. There was a time during the celebration when he was asked to sit in the middle of the dance floor, listening to stories about his life and testimonials of love, affection, and admiration.

My attention was focused on Dad when suddenly, Tata and Grandma Panchita, his parents, gently appeared behind Dad, one at each shoulder. I use the word "gently," because as their forms slowly filtered in, the essence of that energy was ever so gentle and soft. I can only describe it as an all-enveloping, incredibly loving sense. Grandma Panchita, especially, was beaming as she looked at Dad with the most wonderful sense of motherly love. They looked youthful, like photos I have seen when they were in their early thirties (they were in their sixties when they died).

I couldn't believe my eyes! I was astonished and quickly looked around the sea of over a hundred faces, peering intently to see if anyone else saw them too. When I glanced back to Dad, my Grandma Panchita and Tata were gone. Oh, how I wished I would not have looked away from where they were standing. I wonder what would have happened?

Then there was the experience with my cousin Jeannette's son and her late ex-husband. In 1975, my gorgeous eighteen-year-old cousin Jeannette married a handsome guy named Fred, not much older than her. They had a darling baby boy, Jason. They were both very young, and eventually they separated and proceeded to get a divorce. One night, Fred attempted to sneak in through the bedroom window of the house. Jeanette's boyfriend was there. In the dark, he grabbed a gun, thinking Fred was an intruder. Sadly, in the screaming and struggling that ensued, the gun went off. Fred was dead.

When Jason was four, he was diagnosed with a brain aneurysm and fell into a coma. He and Jeannette had been in Victorville visiting family. Jason was having fun doing gymnastics in the backyard with the other children when he came into the house and told his mom he had a headache. She went with him to the bedroom, telling him to lie down and relax. Jeannette wanted to check if he had a fever or something, and asked him to turn over. Jason responded that he couldn't move. "Can you stand?" she asked. He answered that his feet and hands were asleep.

Within ten minutes, Jason became unconscious. The paramedics were called and after stabilizing him, told Jeannette that it appeared he'd had a sudden brain bleed. They would have to take him by helicopter to Children's Hospital in Los Angeles, about eighty-five miles southeast. There was no room for Jeannette in the helicopter, so she had to drive down to L.A. Imagine the anxiety she must have felt!

Jason remained in a coma for three weeks. After the aneurysm burst, the doctors had put him into a medical-induced coma. They wanted to keep him as still as possible, allowing the blood in his brain to reabsorb and release the pressure. They were trying to prevent permanent damage, if not death. If Jason started to wake up, he would holler out that he was in pain. "Mommy, mommy, my head hurts!" They would give him increased sedation, putting him back into a twilight sleep.

One evening, I went to the hospital to visit little Jason. Auntie Stella, Jason's grandma, was there along with Jeannette. The three of us did not say much at all. We prayed and just sat and looked at each other. I reached out and gently started stroking Jason's head. The words "I miss my dad" flashed across my mind. It was as if my hand touching Jason's head transmitted his words to me. The sensation was so strong it took me aback. I did not mention any of this to Auntie or Jeannette.

After visiting for a bit longer, I left the hospital and began the drive home in my cute white 240Z Datsun sports car that Toby had given me for our first Christmas. Boy, did I love that car! The sunroof open, I was buzzing down the dark, empty L.A. freeway, blasting K-Earth 101, enjoying my rock-n-roll. I wanted to shake the intensity of that moment with Jason. I knew I had received communication from him. I just did not know what to think about it, nor what to do about it. I decided there was nothing I could do about it.

Suddenly, out of the corner of my right eye, I felt, and yet simultaneously saw, this "something" come blasting through the sunroof and blow into the passenger seat. I looked over and it was Fred, Jason's dad. I did a double take.

It is difficult to express my conflicting thoughts and emotions. For one thing, we start talking, but I noticed my mouth wasn't moving. Also, it seemed completely natural that we would be cruising the L.A. freeway together this night with the sunroof down. And finally, I'd just been to see his kid, my little nephew, who could be dying and who had just communicated directly to me that he missed his dad!

I turned my head to look at Fred and asked, "What are you doing here?" He did not answer. He looked shy and embarrassed. I guess that would be normal for anyone who had just come crashing through someone's sunroof and plopped into their bucket seat un-invited. Interestingly, Fred's body had a certain amount of opaque substance to it, as I could barely make out the door and window frame of the passenger side as I stared at him.

It was weird that it did not seem strange to see him. It was just a surprise, as you would be surprised if someone showed up at your door unannounced. I told him of Jason's message to me, that he missed his dad, and that Fred needed to stay with him. I asked that he please go and be with his son. It seemed Fred needed reassurance that it was alright to go to Jason. Having just been with Jason, I knew unequivocally it was the right thing.

I distinctly remember looking deep into Fred's eyes for a few seconds when speaking of Jason. Fred looked sad. "Go to him, he needs you," I repeated. I remember having to repeat it because Fred didn't seem to believe what I was saying, as if it could not be true. Now remember, I was driving all this time, speaking and looking at Fred for a minute or so at a time, while simultaneously keeping my eyes on the road. (Later that night, I mused how that could be possible.) The next time I turned to look at Fred, I was alone. My reaction to Fred's visit was a big fat zero. I have a pattern of this emotional zero to these types of events. Classic case of denial.

Then there was Grandma Rosie's surgically documented near death situation. When Grandma Rosie had her colon cancer surgery, Toby and I were living just south of San Francisco at the time. Due to a work and university schedule conflict, I was unable to fly down to Los Angeles to be with her and my mom during this time. On the morning of Grandma Rosie's surgery, I settled myself into the comfortable chair in the middle of our living room. In front of the expansive bay window overlooking the beautiful lush hillside, I prayed and meditated during the time I knew she would be having her surgery.

I closed my eyes and went deep inside myself. I wanted to somehow give her strength by concentrating on sending her all my love. I have no idea how much time went by before I opened my eyes. In front of me on the telephone wire sat a gray dove, staring at me. Never before, or since then, had a dove ever appeared anywhere around here that I saw.

In those summer days when I'd stay with Grandma and Granpappy, it was wonderful to wake up to the cooing of doves, a previously unfamiliar sound to me. When I saw that dove on the telephone wire, it confirmed that Grandma and I were deeply connecting in that moment and everything was on track. Or so I thought.

Much later, my mom shyly shared a story. Seems that during the surgery, Grandma Rosie "died." The anesthesiologist told Mom, "I thought for sure we'd lost her. She's quite a fighter." He continued that there were no vital signs, no blood pressure, no heartbeat. They could not revive her. They were going to declare her dead when finally she came around. Her short-term memory was affected after that, and she was very irritable and quick to get upset.

Later, while Grandma was recovering, she told Mom what happened. Grandma Rosie started with the point that it was much "nicer" where she was going. The music was so beautiful, and she felt "free." She was excited because she was on her way to see Jesus.

She then realized she wasn't going to make it to see Jesus, and she felt "slower" (her words). She was falling. At that moment, she became so angry she couldn't stand it! (Again, her words.) And that is why, she explained to Mom, she'd been cranky ever since. She had to wait.

Not long after Grandma Rosie died, my mom had an "episode" with her, which Mom hesitantly told me about. Mom had been sitting quietly, thinking of Grandma. Grandma's picture suddenly "flew off the wall," to quote Mom. My mom was emphatic when she then went on to detail that the picture did not just fall straight down as if the string on the back of the photo had snapped. Mom insisted that it literally went flying across the room. And wanted to know from me how that was possible. She would never talk about it again.

Dreams and animals can seem to be vehicles of communication between this reality and the "Beyond." I know of a young woman who, when she was sixteen, was driving a car with her best friend and two other friends in the car. The young woman ran a yellow light as a semitruck driver ran his red light, smashing into their car. Her three friends died while she only sustained minor injuries. It is hard to imagine the grief and guilt this young woman had gone through. That was almost five years ago when she told me this story.

Her best friend was absolutely crazy about mermaids, just loved them. This young woman acquaintance recently had had a dream that she was swimming in the ocean, and her best friend swam up to her. Her friend was a mermaid with a tail! She called out her dead friend's name and said, "I'm so sorry, I'm so sorry!" Her best friend waved and said, "I'm fine, it's okay." Then her friend mermaid turned and swam away into a golden light. This young woman, in her early twenties, felt at peace after that.

From Hippocrates to Jung, Tibetan traditions, the ancient Egyptians, the millennia-old Mayans, and many other cultures, they all have a tradition of dreaming and dream interpretations. Some traditions include the belief that dreams could be communications from our loved ones from the "OtherSide." Whether it was this young woman's psychological way of finally coming to peace with the circumstances of her best friend's death, or she really had a visit from her best friend—does it really matter? The young woman was healed from a terrible burden.

If someone shares a dream with you, or what they feel is a communication from someone who has passed, the most meaningful response might be, "Tell me about it." And then, just listen.

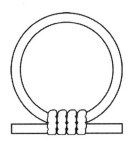

PART IV

Shamanic Experiences
at Power Places®

Lost in the Land of the Maya

Growing up, my summer visits to Grandma Rosie and Grand-pappy's provided quiet space and alone time for me. These wonderful summer visits inadvertently allowed a peek into life lived naturally with intuition. In a tiny valley tucked up against Mount Washington in Highland Park, California, Grandma and Grandpappy had a small, one-and-a-half-story stucco with a basement that made it two stories from the back. The backyard was surrounded on three sides by a hill. On the left was a terraced garden area—both with wild and also cultivated parts. Watering down the dirt in the hot L.A. summer afternoons, the wonderful rich smell of the dirt steaming up, the cooling mist when the breeze shifted, all contributed to a peaceful sense of being alive. These were special events with Grandma Rosie. My senses were heightened during these moments.

Everyone is born with and naturally has abilities of intuition. Grandma Rosie did not so much teach me about intuition as she provided the environment and milieu that demonstrated how other realms of existence are part and parcel of everyday life and living. It was just a normal way to live.

She would listen for communications, for example, from the birds that would come to her garden for food and water. The acknowledgement that other frequencies of communications exist is couched in the folkloric traditions and spirituality of the ancient native peoples of old Mexico. Combined with being a staunch Catholic, she knew that miracles happen, and that the grace of God can manifest. Her life was living proof of that. The possibility of some future miracle was not denied; it was a fact.

I was turning forty-one and it was more important than turning forty. If you plan correctly and cover all the angles and corners at least for a couple of years in advance, the downside of turning forty-one makes turning the big 4-0 a breeze. Your nonplussed attitude about the big 4-0 really upsets everyone on THAT side of the big 4-0. It is very irritating to them that you are not one of the ones who has been sucked down the vortex about getting older. So why not celebrate the freedom of turning forty-one?

For my forty-first birthday I wanted to have a special private celebration. It was an intangible desire that had become a little louder every day for the weeks leading up to this day. Internally, I felt as good as twenty-five. I wanted an adventure with myself on that day. I had no idea that I would receive one of the most important gifts of my life. A full baptism into Intuition. Intuition, the radar of spirit.

I had the inspiration for my birthday present while conducting one of our group tours of the ancient Mayan temples and sites in the Yucatan and Palenque in the eastern part of Mexico. During the previous day's experiences at the ruins of Palenque, my plan began to formulate. Of course, Palenque, powerful ceremonial city of the mysterious Mayas. What a special place to spend my birthday morning!

The Mayan civilization was around for approximately 1500 years, from 1200 B.C to 250 A.D. They are remembered for their advanced civilization and culture that were unequaled in Europe at the time. As a matter of fact, modern architects would be hard-pressed to duplicate a Maya pyramid with its orientation to the solstices and equinoxes even to this day, or of their astronomical skills and the accuracy of their observatories.

Being of Mexican heritage, I have always felt very close to the Maya culture and people, both historically and contemporarily. Where better to have my own private birthday celebration than at the place of my ancestors?

I awoke at dawn, gathered my water and snack food, and took the earliest bus from town to the site. The tingle of tense excitement tickled the underside of my skin like tiny feathers gone wild. The twenty-minute ride from town to the site seemed much longer than usual. I gripped the floor-to-ceiling pole with all my might. I was excited, happy with the fact that the morning adventure lay in front of me. The group had the morning free and I planned to be back at the hotel long before our twelve-noon meeting time. Little did I know that by that time, I would not be the same person who had left the hotel.

Happy as a clam in a calm sea, I surveyed the entrance to that Power Place® known as Palenque. Palenque was a major ceremonial site with a powerful dream chamber and was known throughout ancient Maya land as the location of a great mystery school and a place of hidden knowledge. In years past, I had spent many contented hours here. As much as I was inspired and drawn to this spot, clearly I had another goal in mind today. I had my sights set on the top of the hill.

An unexcavated temple was up there. Usually one needed a guide with a machete to lead the way. It seemed incredibly special to go to an unexcavated ceremonial place for my birthday. Get myself there to the base of the low mountain in one of the local jeeps for hire, then jump off at the side of the mountain. Without the help of a guide, I'd go to the top! I knew I could do it. I would go straight up the mountain in a straight line, walk across the top and then straight down the other side of the mountain. Once on the other side, I'd be able to clearly pick up the trail that made its way back to the foursquare plaza by the main temple in Palenque. I'd keep my eye on the Maya sun and go in a straight line, no matter what. Piece of cake, right?

I reached for my compass on the approach to the drop-off point. I'd pick the spot at the bottom of the mountain that seemed halfway around the hill. I had forgotten the compass in the excitement of packing for my adventure. I quickly calculated all my options. 1. I knew where I was. 2. I knew where I was going. 3. I had plenty of time before needing to get back to the hotel. 4. I had already walked this far. 5. It was either forget the whole thing, go back to the road that went to the ruins and come up with something else, go back to the hotel, find someone who had a compass (highly unlikely), or get a guide with a machete, defeating the purpose of my birthday morning adventure/celebration. In the moment, my calculations dangerously failed to consider that this mountain was blocking the easterly rising sun, on which I was depending to be my compass.

I decided to go for it; I can do this. And so my right foot dressed up in my New Balance tennis shoe stepped off the path and onto the slope of the hill. No way was I turning back now! This was fun;

it felt incredible to be alive; and every tree, bush, and leaf in the rainforest seemed to say welcome to the neighborhood!

I was so bent on concentrating and watching my step that it was not until fifteen minutes into the straight climb up when the reality check started to slowly filter down, like the sweat on my brow. Teri, this is a rainforest. That means bushes and trees all grow together, closely. Elementary. What that means is that it is physically impossible to go in a straight line. In reality, I knew I currently was not in a straight line from the path I had left.

I evaluated my situation. Even if I went back to the trail, I would not have enough time to start all over before having to meet my group. True, once I got to the top and in view of the sun, it would be easy to evaluate my situation and determine which direction would get me back to the foursquare plaza. I decided to keep on heading up or at least go as straight up as I could go.

Now it was no longer fun. It was a difficult job to complete. The hill was pretty much vertical with a tangle of trees, vines, and bushes obscuring any easy places with secure footing. I would grab a sapling or a limb, test it by putting some weight on it, throw my foot up, plant it as firmly in the soil above as I could with one to two feet of mulch underneath, and haul myself up. I literally could not see the forest for the trees and bushes.

My hands and arms, legs and shoes, become filthy, scratched up, and battered. I got into the rhythm of the haul up, not deciding what tree to tackle next until the moment I had to make the decision of where to plant my foot. Pretty much, I based my decision on how straight a line I could proceed with, and what bit of rainforest sod or particular tree and its roots would support my weight. Without the brush and trees of the rainforest, I could have found a much easier footing up, with rocky ledges, natural protrusions, and leveled areas.

I had decided to "take the mountain" this birthday morning, and so be it. I don't remember glancing once at my watch; time of completion was not an issue in the moment. I became more confident, I felt strong and good about myself, and I could haul myself up hills by swinging from tree roots and trunks at the age of forty-one. It just goes to show you how misplaced our perceptions can be, and how blind we can be to those misperceptions.

Why do I say that? Because in the glory of the moment, one thing had not sunk in yet … I was hopelessly lost. No one in the entire world knew where I was, including myself! To my group, I was probably leisurely enjoying a cafecito in my room. In reality, one of the hardest lessons of my life was unfolding before my eyes.

What I had calculated to be optically the last quarter of the way up the top of the flattened mountaintop kept receding with every step. Like an oasis in the desert. I just stayed with the next step and trees in front of me because I was confident that once I reached the top, all would be clear and smooth after that. I'd probably even have time for a late breakfast before having to meet the group. Wrong on all counts.

My now very dusty New Balances finally flipped themselves onto the top of the hill. I came crashing through the peripheral ring of brush. I was not expecting such a wide swath of brush and thought the flattened hilltop would have more easily revealed the old temple ruins. Checking the sky, I could barely make out the sun's diffuse presence through the high gray clouds and heavy low mist overhead.

"Great," I thought, there goes the 'Right Eye of God' compass

I'd been planning on using. It was quickly dawning on me that my other major reference point, the unexcavated temple that I'd been depending on, was not here. I mean I couldn't see it. Surveying my surroundings, I saw brush, tiny stones, and small sapling trees and vines scattered about. No temples, ruins, excavated blocks, old stone walls, nothing.

Bear in mind, at this point I was taken aback by the unexpected sight of what greeted me up there. The scenario I'd planned on was not happening a whit. My complete lack of direction and limited visibility to less than one foot in front of me jerked my brain around and plunged it into a confusion that felt as if it was tripping over itself.

I temporarily distracted myself with the thought of how disappointed I was that the special private birthday ceremony at this ancient temple was not to be. The second distracting thought was that the group leader would kill me if I was late for our twelve o'clock departure time. She was a "piece of work" and had been increasingly demanding the last couple of days, necessitating all my diplomatic skills to keep her from turning nasty.

I stood my ground with my dusty shoes firmly under me; I did not move. The jungle sounds of the local non-human inhabitants filled my ears. The drone of multiple insects, a few scattered birdcalls, were all I could hear. The rest was a stillness that, under other circumstances, I would have found luscious. The wind was completely asleep.

I was lost, 100 percent lost. The jungle extends for hundreds of miles with only a few scattered villages. I had no clue which way to go. What were the odds of hitting the skinny trail that goes back around to the Palenque ruins and site? Not good at all. If I walked across the top and down the wrong way, it would be a lot worse. Okay, I thought, sooner or later, someone will come up here. It was more likely the latter scenario. Or, I could just wait. Or, I could start hollering and yelling for help—how embarrassing!

I checked my canteen; I could last one and a half days in the shade. It was August, so the nights were not cold. I'd get bitten to death by insects … I refused to think about the snakes. I finally decided on my course of action after reviewing the not-so-pleasant options. New Balance would take me one step at a time back to my base, back to my Palenque.

Now here comes the key to everything. The moment, the main moment, one asks oneself a question at least once in their life. A moment that can define one's future for even decades.

What do I do? Which way do I go from here?

Being at an ancient site of holiness for people gone into the clouds of the past always brought a sense of stillness to me. A stillness that bathed me in a pool of connection to my surroundings, within myself, and life at large. I always felt "home" in the nurturing, uplifting, and sheltering way a safe "home" was meant to convey.

My mind was reeling from the fact that no temple of grandeur met my eyes here. There were no walls, not even any rubble to be seen, because of all the vegetation. This area was much larger than I thought. There was a growing, but still manageable, worry inside. Now this was the real problem. The jungle growth up here was not as high as the trees when I was climbing up. Still, the ground was obscured and so were any other possible landmarks. Looking overhead, the sun was lost behind a thick shield of gray clouds and mist.

In hindsight, I can look at this naiveté and foolishness and say, "What the heck was I thinking putting myself into this situation? No compass, no map, no guide, no clue. Only some wish to go to a ceremonial place to have a private prayer on my birthday morning." I am usually a prepared yet spontaneous person. I certainly know how to get around pretty much anywhere under any sort of circumstances.

Why this, why now? I know I wanted to do something very special; I know I wanted it to be ceremonial. I guess I had also given myself a dare, the kind we throw down as kids to each other. I dare you, at age forty-one, to go traipsing into the jungle to locate a little sunrise temple that most guides don't even know about, find it, have a ceremony, come back, and return to the group at the hotel, and no one will ever know. This will be your own little secret.

I was stripped of all direction, visual assistance of landmarks, and paths and trails. I stood there and contemplated my situation. If I chose the wrong way, the jungle went on and on and on. If I waited for someone to eventually come up here, who knows how long that would be. I could wait until the sun came through the mist to determine what was west and what was east. I knew I had to head southwest to get to my Palenque. Or I could start walking with my best guess. If you can believe it, my worst fear was that I did not want to face the group leader's wrath. She had me bamboozled. Of all the scary stuff happening in the moment, the thought of being late and having to face her "Kali/human devouring/spit you out" anger was the scariest thing of all!

That did it. I decided to take my chances and get off this mountain. Fine, BUT which way to go? I slowed myself down, gathered all my senses, quieted my breathing, stilled my mind. I'd tune into the right direction, and use my intuition to point the way. Simple. My intuition did not point out the right way, so on my part, I received back a big fat zero of information. Up until now, I had given great store to my intuition, my little voice inside, my gut feeling or whatever you wish to call it. Past experience also showed me that I had to be objective to the information returning, unattached and open. This is very important. I also had repeatedly experienced that it was much easier to sense something or ask a question on someone else's behalf and receive a clear answer. Much easier than it was to receive clarity for oneself!

I had to find a way off this mountain. I was fully stopped in my tracks, giving my full attention. What decision had I made to get me up here in the first place? Was it my "gut feeling," "that little voice," that landed me here? If the answer to any of this is yes, then absolutely this intuition thing is under suspicion.

I must admit that intuition or the sixth sense or whatever one wishes to call it had been of service in varying degrees pretty much my whole life. Mostly cultivated by examples from my dear Grandma Rosie and reinforced over the years by instances too numerous to count.

We all can recall instances of thinking of someone out of the blue, the phone rings, and it's the person on the line. We think to ourselves that it's a "coincidence," or think nothing at all. Well, my Grandma Rosie treated these coincidences or serendipitous happenings as perfectly natural and normal in the course of events. This attitude rubbed off on me. It wasn't until I entered my mid–twenties, during the whole seventies introduction of Eastern philosophy and metaphysics to the West, that I began a more formal cultivation of intuition or one's "tuner inner" as it is referred to in our house. Over the years, I had developed my own style of intuition, which more or less comes forward when called upon. I deliberately use the words "more or less" as there had been plenty of times I really did not know what this process consisted of.

All right, here I go. I took some deep breaths, closed my eyes, and felt myself calming down. This intuition thing would and could work to get me out of this jam. My worst nightmare was to face the wrath of that woman, so I had to get off this hill and to the hotel. It is difficult to put into exact words the experience of intuition, the other "sense," the gut feeling. If it has happened to you, you already know. If it hasn't, or more likely you did not recognize it for what it was, you wouldn't really understand here. If I had to describe it, the words would simply be "my awareness."

I use the term awareness to imply a "heightened" sense of perception. Any intense emotion or critical or intense moment can bring in that "heightened" sense of perception or awareness. Add to that the desire to know something at a level beyond just our brain or our mind.

With absolutely no sense of direction and just about zero visibility, I could not depend on my five senses. I wanted to know which way, which direction, to get off this jungle mountain. I did my usual get-centered routine, took a deep breath and let my senses totally open up, and just get deeply quiet inside. Usually this is how I proceed with my meditations. This also works when I want to "tune into" something or "feel" something out. I did what I normally do. I was getting no sense of what direction to take. Feeling at one with the environment and an overall connection was not helping me at all!

I guess I was not surprised. I thought just maybe I was more panicky than I realized and was blocking my intuition from feeding back to me what I needed to know. As I internally scanned myself, I was not aware of being panicky or fearful. I was just not getting the information I needed, or so I thought!

You know the old saying, "It was right in front of my nose the whole time?" That is exactly what happened to me next. The answer proved to be literally just right in front of my nose the whole time. I became aware that what I did know was that it felt right to take one step in a certain direction and then just stop. And so I did.

Then I sensed where to take the next step. And so I did, and then just stood still. Feeling around, I then "felt" where to take the next step. And so I did. By this time, I could feel my "chi," or life force, really going though me. I directed it to flow out of my hands and out the top of my head. I raised my arms, palms outward, directing my life energy to the trees around me. At a certain point in my scanning, I would feel what can be described as a "density." It was toward that exact "dense" spot that I would take my next step and then halt again.

This is how my "New Balance" feet team and I proceeded, one baby step, stop, feel it, another baby step, stop, feel it, for the next two hours or so. I was completely immersed in this process. Not judging or in fear, only going with the flow. By the time the sun was almost overhead, I was down the mountain and in a ravine. The dry riverbed held no markers as to which way a stream would flow, which would have been helpful in indicating direction. The canopy of trees allowed the sun's rays to stream through, yet still hid the location of my missing compass, the sun. I had no idea which direction my Palenque was. One thing was certain. At this point, it was no longer in the original direction I had set out for in the early morning.

I continued step by step, as if I was someone blind with a cane gently tapping the ground with my New Balance team, and feeling myself out of this one. And then, a female voice, way off in the distance. Riveted to my spot, I became a gigantic five-foot-seven ear as I literally strained out of my skin to make out where the heck that voice was coming from. Silence.

Stubbornness and pride prevented me from shouting out. Egos are such a trip and so interesting. No way was I going to holler out like some wimp or baby and break the silence. Silence. I kept going, baby-step, baby-step. Silence greeted me in between the baby-steps as I continued to pause to direct my hands toward the trees, sensing the right way to go.

The normal-sounding female voice bored into my eardrums. Close enough to decipher that it was female, yet too far to make out the words. Silence. A muffled footstep. I looked up and there she was coming around the bend up on an indecipherable trail approximately twenty feet above me. With the golden light of the sun falling on her cropped Nordic blond hair, fair skin, and long legs held in khaki hike shorts, she was a goddess. She was saying something to someone who was around the bend and not quite visible.

So ordinary a scene. Hikers meeting on trails, enjoying time out in nature. She saw me. I remember staring at her and then mumbling something about how far to the ruins. She clearly said something that my brain just whizzed in and out. Thank goodness she pointed which way to go.

She and her friend continued on the trail. I waited down in the riverbed until they passed and all was silent again. Then I climbed up from the riverbed, through the ravine and up to the small, barely sixteen-inch-across trail hugging the mountain that they had just been on. Carefully and speedily, I moved along the flat trail, my New Balance twins sounding confident on the smooth dirt trail.

Eventfully, the field of banana trees and huge ferns provided a familiar landmark. I was on the backside of my Palenque. Quietly, I pushed aside frond after frond, now being able to see only six inches in front of me at a place where the fronds were so thick. The final banana frond raised like a curtain, revealing the exquisite Temple of the Inscriptions and the lush plaza of grass in front of it.

I walked onto the grass and lay down, stretching out luxuriously as if I had just returned from a glorious, relaxing hike. I was pleased that everything felt so normal. I inhaled the wonderful peaceful energy of the place.

Reality set in. The last lap of this birthday mission lay like a stream full of alligators in front of me. The highest priority was getting the bus and taxis necessary to make quick connections back to the hotel before Kali/Medusa released her wrath, blasting me to smithereens.

Now, those of you who have had a chance to visit the exquisitely beautiful and fascinating country that is Mexico know that "quick" is not in the vocabulary of this wonderful nation. That, however, is part of its magnificent charm and why Mexico provides such an incredible haven for us frenzied, microwave Norte Americanos.

Swiftly I zeroed in on the path that snaked through the middle of the Palenque site and was off. I did not even glance at any of the wondrous buildings of this mystical place as I made my way through to the side entrance where it was easier to get a bus already on the return route to town.

Sure enough, shortly, a van pulled up albeit already loaded. I threw myself almost in front of it and on the mercy of the driver who was already shaking his head no. In Spanish, I explained my predicament, that I had a group that would be expecting me by twelve noon, etc. He shrugged and jerked his head, indicating I could get in.

Phase One check, I thought to myself. I glanced at my watch for the first time that morning. 11:34 a.m. Yes, I would just barely make it. On purpose, I had not looked at my watch previously until this moment. I figured it would just have increased my anxiety and would not have made things happen faster anyway. In other words, my experience, getting lost … it was what it was.

Now, it is what it is. I was coming into the home stretch. I was going to make it! Arriving into town, I quickly thanked the driver, tipped him my gratitude, jumped out of the public van, and grabbed the first taxi. In Spanish, I told the guy to make it to the hotel post haste. It was still a good ten minutes out of town with normal driving. He made it in eight.

I envisioned everyone, it was just wishful thinking, having a relaxing morning in their free time enjoying the pool or shopping. As the taxi made its way down the driveway of the hotel, I had already calculated quickly running to my room and grabbing my gear for the day's outing. I wasn't paying attention to what was in front of me at the entrance of the hotel.

It was only when the driver stopped that I turned and focused on the sight that greeted me. My entire group stood there, huddled together on the curb, looking scared. My eyes shifted twenty feet to the right and there stood the blond Kali/Medusa ... My worst nightmare was unfolding. I swear there were flames blazing out of her eyes, steam coming out of her ears. In another time, she would have said, "Off with her head" and I would have been history.

I glanced again at the group way over on the other side, jumped out of the taxi, ran up to Kali and asked, "What's wrong?" She said in a cold, steely voice that was like laser surgery on my brain, that the hotel bus shuttle to and from town wasn't working, and for some reason, taxis were not available. There wasn't anyone available at the hotel to do anything about it and people had been stuck at the hotel.

I went over to the group and they all just stared at me and nodded. Couldn't get a straight answer out of anyone. Kali/Medusa had tied their tongues up in knots.

With my heart pounding, I walked into the hotel and spoke to the head of reception. Yes, no problem. He could get a taxi shuttle to come and take us to town to catch the local bus that made the daily round trip to Agua Azul waterfalls. It would be here in fifteen minutes. He did not know how long it would take for the hotel shuttle to be fixed, so we should plan on getting ourselves back from town at the end of the day. He also had no idea why there had been a problem with getting a taxi from town. Maybe for an hour or less because of many people going to Sunday Mass, but that was it.

I returned to the front of the hotel to convey this latest news to everyone. Just as Perseus in Greek mythology avoided looking into the eyes of Medusa and thus didn't turn to stone, I did the same. I avoided her eyes. No one spoke. I made small talk to break the tension as we waited for the taxi van from town.

It was strange indeed to go from what my experience had been the whole morning to this scenario. These moments unfolding were unreal and surrealistic. To be honest, they were flat, linear, superficial, and mundane. In the time of being lost in the rainforest, I had lived in a place inside myself that was connected to everything around me. There was a fullness and multi-dimensionality to that experience that made this moment pretty lame.

The rest of the day unfolded uneventfully. The exception was the incredible Power Place® of Agua Azul waterfalls. It was an ancient Mayan ceremonial place of purification where the elements sparkled with wonderful healing energies. A potent place of assimilation for a pilgrim who had passed an important initiation.

It was sometime later that I realized that since being lost in the jungle, my intuition had become as natural as breathing. I was consciously using it all the time; it was reflexive. No longer second-guessing it or making it turn into what I thought I wanted the answer to be. I just trusted.

Ever since my New Balance experience over twenty years ago, I have further cultivated, nurtured, honed, and consciously sought at every opportunity to develop this natural ability everyone is born with. Why? Trusting my intuition, my gut feeling, provides a life that can be easier in many ways, less negative unwanted surprises, as I have been "forwarned" so to speak. A little easier, and a freer life.

Machu Picchu: Where You Meet Yourself Around Every Corner

E ver since Toby and I first gazed upon those wondrous edifices mysteriously and sensually peeking out from the lush jungle on top of the granite mountain, I'd dreamed of spending the night inside Machu Picchu. I had told Walter, our dear Peruvian friend and Power Places'® director of tours, not to wait for me at the gate when Machu Picchu closed at 6 p.m. I would not be leaving. I was finally going to do it. Spend the night alone in the "Crystal City." For years, I expected and hoped that the night in front of me would be one of the highest "peak experiences" in my life. What it turned out to be was the scariest, most uncomfortable, and longest night of my life! However, I learned and will never forget one of those universal truths we need to learn in life and that is: "You get what you ask for."

After so many years of taking multiple groups into Machu Picchu, I knew exactly what to pack for my overnight bag. I hate to be cold, and up in the mountains, the temperature could plunge to almost freezing. I had no idea what "spiritual" adventures awaited me that night; however, whatever they turned out to be, I was going to be warm and toasty experiencing them!

I was ready to confront and face my fears now, all at once, and I could "take" it. Take what, the process? I was ready to let go, in a big way, and take it in in a big way. I was coming from my heart, curious, enthusiastic, and feeling courageous.

At the window of my hotel room right next to the entrance, "Intitaytanchi," Father Sun in the ancient Inca tongue of Quechua, showed me it was early afternoon. The mountain peaks seemed only an arm's length away. What an adventure I was about to start. I felt confident, happy, safe and secure, warm, and comfy ... oh my heart was singing! I was going to spend the night in the arms of this Mother Mountain I loved so much. What better place to face one's fears than from the safety of your mother's lap? Nothing can harm you.

It is difficult to describe the huge sense of comfort and "welcome home" feeling I receive every single time I enter that ancient Power Place® known as Machu Picchu. Every cell in my body seems to vibrate the same message ... "What a relief, I made it, I'm home, I'm safe, I'm happy and secure, I'm glad to be alive." Could this be heaven? Is this what the heavenly state is like, I wonder? Is this what is meant by "Heaven on Earth?" If there is a place that satisfies that criteria, it is Machu Picchu.

An external place, person, or thing can cause the above described internal cognitive and emotional feeling based on biochemical states that occur. In actuality, Power Places® were built by the ancients to do just this. Amplify our awareness within. Yet yogis and mystics, with decades of inner training and meditation, can be sitting on a rock on the freeway in downtown Los Angeles during rush hour, and they can reach these internal states. Neuroscientists say it is only the brain neurotransmitters sending "feel good" chemicals like endorphins and dopamine pouring out into the brain and nervous system that cause these emotions and states of the psyche. True. However whether the structures of a Power Place® such as Machu Picchu or the Great Pyramid are amplifying our "inner" state, or the yogis are self activating their "inner" state, there is no denying something out of the ordinary is occurring.

I was eagerly anticipating this upcoming night safe in the arms of The Mother while facing all my fears. I happily went about making my final preparations, like a kid getting ready for a camping trip. How delicious anticipation is as a child, how uncomplicated. One is free to enjoy excitement without "baggage." At least I was as a child. My parents provided the sort of environment where we kids experienced the "magic of kidhood" pretty often.

I had asked Walter not to mention to anyone my plan to stay. It was important to me that no one knew, that no one would be thinking of me and sending their thoughts to me as I was inside that night. Surveying my room to make sure I had all I needed, I noticed I was boiling hot. I had on three shirts, including a polypropylene one, one pair of long johns, one sweater, and thick cotton long pants and a pair of tights. Also in my bag were a red Australian fine wool cape, llama blanket, two extra pairs of sweatpants, two extra sweaters, three woolen scarves, llama gloves (two pairs), two pairs of llama socks, a llama hat, and a bottle of water. I was reassured that no matter what was in store in facing my demons of fear, I was going to be warm as I looked into the whites of their eyes!

I decided I was not going to take food and neither would I take a watch, so that I could not "check" the time. (Checking our watches and clocks always pulls us out of "the flow" of the moment. If we are in "the flow" and aware and sensitive to it, we'll sense when the moment or time is up anyway.)

Leaving my room, I joined my group at the broad concrete stairs by the kiosk that makes up the tourist entrance to the Machu Picchu ruins. We were going in for our second visit this afternoon. Around 3 p.m., the sun starts to set behind the mountain and the breeze may come up. It can be chilly in the afternoon at this time of year, so it was not surprising that I carried a bag of gear. Silently, I asked the "Guardians of the place" permission to enter into their home of Machu Picchu. We all trudged the dirt and Inca stone path, making our way to the entrance to the ancient city.

The five-minute walk from the kiosk where tickets are purchased to the actual entrance provides a transition from the ordinary to the extraordinary world. The sound becomes gradually muffled as you make your way from the kiosk, away from the people, shuttle buses, the afternoon Peruvian music, and just the commotion of civilization. Walking down the steps, your hands instinctively go to the walls, your eyes wanting to simultaneously check the positioning of your feet and absolutely soak in the heavenly, majestic, and take-your-breath-away view of the blue-blue sky, green-green mountains, and appropriately placed mystical-looking mist.

On the left, the high wall of the lush terraced mountain hugged me as I made my way. On the right, the gorgeous, lush panoramic view of the surrounding mountain peaks always takes my breath away. I stop dead in my tracks every time, even after all these years, and all these times of entering. One passes through two small rooms immediately before entering the site. The Inca walls are about six-and-a-half feet high, and the laid-out Incan stones of the floor are smooth, worn, and with an uneven surface.

The stone walls and thatched roofs and narrowing laby-rinth-like space contribute to that sense of going into another world. Squeezing between the last two huge boulders and having to bow a bit conveys the humility, respect, and state of awareness one needs when entering a sacred space.

The sun had already set behind the mountain peaks as the guard blew his whistle, announcing it was almost 6 p.m. and the gate would be closing. As usual, he went around the site checking for stragglers and peeking into possible hiding places. After all these years, I know this Machu Picchu place like I know every curve of my own sweet mother's face. I had slipped over and down to the far northwestern side of the place and settled down comfortably under a rocky overhang. I knew the guard had no incentive to check way down over there.

Is it possible to be peaceful and have your heart pound at the same time? I leaned back into the granite rock that felt like a comfortable chair and stared at the rim of the rugged mountain range. The white golden light of the sun behind the mountains outlined the deep purple black of the now sunless three thousand foot high monolithic hunks. The only sounds were the far-below river making its way around three-fourths of the base of the mountain, various exotic insects zipping by, and the last of the swifts, darting around in one last attempt to catch dinner. The air was completely still, and I felt still, except for the pounding of my heart.

Earlier that afternoon, I had asked that "all my fears be revealed tonight in Machu Picchu so I would be free!" This epitome of egotistical stupidity was an example of spiritual naiveté, with a large dose of exuberance. How "Leo" dramatic to throw one's arms open to the Universe and say, "I am coming in tonight to face all my fears and be free of them."

The millions and trillions of little fears and big fears that my conscious and unconscious possessed had received a wide-open invitation. I was asking that in this holy place they come to light. In only twelve hours, I would be exorcised and exonerated from all these fears in my life. Right … motivation appeared noble for a plan that betrayed my naiveté. What one asks for thou shalt receive, sooner or later. If one asks for anything at a Power Place®, especially during such a propitious time as the evening of the Winter Solstice (and this was the night before the June Solstice, the holiest time of year for the ancient Incas and the Andean native people), one can conceivably immediately get what one asks for. What most people forget is a very important detail; that whatever one *has to go through* to get what they ask for will also come to you!

What does that mean? It means that most of the time in asking for something, we get all kinds of things happening to us or coming our way that we did not ask for. There is no way that we can accurately predict a road if we have never traveled on it before. You can surmise, based on your life's research and experience, but there is no way one can know something until one is actually on that particular road.

So we desire, ask for something to happen, and many surprises also arrive. Why was I wanting now to be freed from my fears in the first place?

At this moment of the "Time Between the Worlds," when the day dissolves into the elixir of night and its promise of other possibilities, I was centered and content. Leaning against a comforting curve of granite, I was breathing, listening, and waiting. Fully present and in my body, I felt ancient somehow, and yet like a child of five, simultaneously. I was in the "Crystal City," and I had all night to enjoy it and be dazzled.

Time passed until there was none. Not having a watch, my only reference to time was the gradually deepening shadow display on the surrounding steep mountainsides. My ears relaxed into the sound of silence moving beyond the distant swoosh of the Sacred River far below. I sat there motionless on the grass, sinking deeper into the granite, the Machu Picchu Sphinx.

I stared, studied, and melded my mind onto the horizon of high craggy mountain peaks that jutted up before me. To this day, I can tell you exactly between which two peaks the sun sets on the eve of June Winter Solstice.

The aloneness was spectacular. Utterly, entirely alone and utterly, entirely besotted with the fact that I was here alone and the luckiest person alive. The world of Dusk dissolved into the world of Night. The familiar landmarks of the temples and buildings by day gave way to the familiar environment dressed in its mysterious nightdress. Now here is what is interesting. Machu Picchu truly becomes alive at night.

I did not stir from my granite easy chair. Wondering where to go off exploring next, I knew the answer as I asked myself that question. What I call the Pachamama (Earth Mother) Stone, of course, would come next. Surefooted and with confidence, I left my rocky throne to cross the far end of the grassy plaza where this carved monolithic rock sat. It greets all those who come to the entrance of the narrow foot trail that goes just about straight up to the top of Huayna Picchu Peak. On either side of the Pachamama Stone, two high-ceiling thatched roof huts, Huayrana-the passage of wind, stand guard.

Initially seeing this gigantic boulder towering up at over fifteen feet, I just wanted to drape myself onto it. The monolithic vertical, almost flat stone was hugely impressive and conveyed a powerful sense of comfort in some way. The brilliant Incas had carved the top in the shape of a puma ready to attack, emulating the shape of Pumasillo mountain peak directly behind it. Standing directly in front of the Pachamama rock altar, the tops of the two peaks aligned perfectly.

The ingenious pre-Inca and Inca architects and astronomers certainly had a heavenly plan in mind with the design of Machu Picchu and its different aspects. This Pachamama stone is an important marker and has its own intricate carving and a special altar at the base. No one knows for sure the purpose. However, logically, the mountain behind it must have been very important to merit its own image plus altar. For me, it's a place to always go to feel grounded and connected.

It made sense that I would go here at the beginning of this night's venture. A place of great familiarity to touch, like a favorite dress, before the long night that lay ahead. I purposely did not bring any books or writing materials. Just as I did not want a watch to distract me from the experience or from myself, so, too, a book, pen, and paper could have been distractions.

Draping myself on my "Rock of Comfort," I waited for the wave of the always forthcoming deep sigh to ripple through me. Nothing. It was like the touchpoint was turned off. I could feel the heat of the day's hot sun in the stone flowing along my entire spine and the back of my legs. This lack of connection to one of my favorite spots in the world coincided with little sparkles of anxiety starting to shoot off my stomach and the back of my neck.

What was I doing here? Spending the night here, for hours, how stupid. No food, only water, stuck until at least 6 a.m. Stuck here, stuck with myself. The guards would open the gate at that time, as I'd gotten special permission for my group to enter for a Solstice sunrise ceremony before the site was open to the public. A free-floating anxiety began to slowly ooze out of my bone marrow, insidiously making its way from one cell to the next.

That sudden dialogue of fear in my head jerked me from a plateau of inner quiet and appreciation of the place to the cacophony of the fast lane in an Indy 500 race. It was mentally not a fear of anything physically happening to me. It was my body acting as if it was in fear of physical danger (heart racing, palms and head sweating, stomach lurching, and my head pounding ... a garden-variety, red-alert adrenaline rush). I had no thoughts of physical danger.

The moon was not yet up over the eastern mountains. However, its presence was already beginning to activate the landscape with reflected silvery light. The temples and ruins responded to its caress by slowly shimmering. It was as if each stone was ever so slowly beginning to wake up, stretch slightly, and begin breathing. One by one, as the moonlight increased and its halo grew stronger on the spot on the eastern mountain it was planning to emerge from, the ruins seemed to awaken from slumber.

As I surveyed this awakening landscape shifting itself out of slumber, I told myself to relax. Relax because there was not anything to this feeling that something or someone was moving around, coming to get me, and their numbers were increasing. It was my imagination. If someone else was there sneaking in as I had, then we certainly wouldn't have to be hiding from each other!

To help me calm down, I went through the checklist in my head as to why no one else would be hiding. There are only three ways (aside from a helicopter flying in) to enter the site of Machu Picchu. The first way is the modern main entrance for tourists. One arrives by train down below. A small, twenty-eight-seater bus snakes its way up fourteen switchbacks to arrive at the modern entrance to the site. Walking in, the mountain is on the left with a sheer cliff on the right. Once the high solid wooden gate at the kiosk is closed, one cannot get out or enter the ruins by this route. Gates are too high, precipices too steep. The second way is hiking the Inca Trail and coming up to the Gateway of the Sun high above the site. This point is considered the original entrance point to the city. One comes over the ridge and suddenly all of Machu Picchu is laid out below you in a visual panoramic feast.

I glanced up in the direction of the Gateway of the Sun. What a moment that must have been centuries ago to be standing there when Machu Picchu was at its height of heavenly powers, earthly splendors, and abundance. Treacherous at night, I'd see flashlights blinking if anyone was coming in that way. The third option in is from the trail coming from the top of Huayna Picchu mountain. (The trademark peak one sees in all the photos of Machu Picchu.) If coming from there, one would have had to spend the day up there. Totally improbable. No one in their right mind who wanted to live would attempt to negotiate that practically straight vertical walk down at night.

I plopped down in the grass on the other side of the "Rock of Comfort" to methodically survey my situation and plan my next move. I was a bit disconcerted that I was not having an experience of energy or inner message or anything spiritual.

True, the night had just begun. The incessant chatter in my head was getting tiresome as old, negative ruminations played their music in the space between my ears. The gamut of self-put-down, self-sabotage, self-dislike, and self-criticism made a dense wall of free-floating anxiety.

I reminded myself this was a test, actually a series of tests. A test of how evolved I had become after all these years on my spiritual path. This was a test of courage, too late to change my mind.

On hindsight, this whole night's episode came down to one basic, mundane revelation. Self-acceptance and self-love. It was not necessary to prove anything to Toby, myself, my family, friends, colleagues, my clients, the teachers and authors I work with, the cosmos or the god/ goddess. Self-love can be mistakenly perceived as a boring or narcissistic concept. Self-love and self-acceptance are what it is about. Or just plain 'ol Enlightened Self-Interest. In the challenge of the personal gauntlet I had thrown down earlier that day, all aspects, without exception, reflected how I constantly flagellate myself at one level or another.

Setting things up so that I could tell myself that tonight I was walking into, not just into a den of pumas (the Andean mountain lion and sacred animal/spirit to the ancient Incas) but into their mouths, which would overnight, somehow, make me an enlightened spiritual person free of fear. And this would make me peaceful and happy inside? And perhaps more loveable?

In this moment, even though the moonlight clearly outlined every blade of grass, none of that altruistic self-enlightened stuff mattered. I was here, scared, literally not able to get out. More accurately, I rather would have died than gone pounding on the gate and screaming to get out. It is doubtful anyone would have heard me anyway as the hotel up here was too far away.

I stood in the main big plaza, an open grassy area in the middle of Machu Picchu. The ceremonial side to the west is where most of the temples are located, with one exception. The opposite east side is where the main living quarters, storage area, and astronomical observatory are, and the Temple to the Condor.

I surveyed the area all around. In my temporary calm state, I instinctively moved off to another of my comfort spots in the place. The Temples to the Wind, Water, Earth, and Sun (fire), the four elements. When in doubt, return to the basics. One cannot get more basic than the four elements. Deliberately, I moved off in that direction, grateful I knew where I was going for at least the next five minutes.

These four small temples converge at a major Power point in the complex. Built in a natural cave, The Temple of Pachamama, representing the earth element (Pacha: earth, mama: mother), sits directly underneath the Sun (Inti) Temple. This Sun Temple is only approximately twenty-five by twenty-five feet, and approximately one and a half stories high. At the Sun Temple/Earth Temple vertical axis, the Temple to the Water (Una in Quechua, the ancient Inca language) sits flush with the Temple to the Wind (Caya: air element).

Out of the four elements, everyone has at least two elements that they deeply connect with. Think about it. Some people have to soak in a tub to feel as if they are in heaven. Or dip into a river to experience nirvana. Others absolutely love the breeze and wind, while others don't even notice it or find it bothersome. Others are attracted to sunlight, and at times, even over-expose themselves. While for others, their favorite activity is going on a picnic and sitting on the grass, or picking a huge boulder to drape themselves over.

What is interesting is that we deeply connect with and seek out those elements that are at some level deficient within our bodies. Always the organism (our bodies) seeks out homeostasis and balance within itself.

The uneasiness and almost palpable sense of overall body contraction was not relieved one bit at this Power Place® of Pachamama that previously had provided endless moments of peace over the years. I could hardly sit still by this time. My throat was tight. I was very irritable and frightened simultaneously, which is a weird sensation. Each minute felt like a week; I had no idea how much longer until sunrise.

It was during this time that unfortunately, I started thinking about the stories I'd heard about people seeing UFOs and maybe even ETs (extraterrestrials) in the Andes. My ear barometer index went up a couple of notches, I must admit. This was a time when the media and certain groups were bringing up ET visits, government conspiracies with ETs, alien abductions, and other such inflammatory drama. It did not matter to me if "they" were out there or not. What did matter was that if they were around, they DID NOT COME TO VISIT ME TONIGHT. NO WAY. They were definitely not invited to my fear-fest. I drew the line there with the Universe as to how far I'd have to go to get my Crystal City "Red Badge of Courage."

I glanced up at the cobalt sky. The intensity of my discomfort for a moment took a backseat to the breathtaking exquisite inverted bowl of twinkling colors known as the Milky Way. In the still of the night with no breeze present, that sight so familiar to anything or anyone that has ever been born, lived, and died ... that sight became everything.

Maybe it was the fact that at 8,600 feet up in the Andes without any pollution, the sky seemed so much closer. Or maybe it was the fact that I was so alone. Or maybe it was the fact that I was so scared. Whatever the reason or combination thereof, I was suddenly very comforted by this blanket of lights that seemed to settle on my shoulders. However, this comfort was to be only of a few breaths' duration.

Out of the corner of my eye, I thought I saw three somethings moving in the sky. I know what you are saying: "It was a satellite, a plane, a shooting star." As I turned my head and stared at the spot in the sky that caught my attention, I could feel my left eye twitch.

Now, "left-eye twitching" is a beacon signal that has occurred only a few times in my life. Extreme duress situations, like at age fifteen telling my parents I was going to see a movie five miles away when in actuality I was off to Hollywood with my girlfriend to cruise Sunset Boulevard and the hot club, Whisky a Go Go. We were followed by a group of guys on the twenty-mile trip home, and we were unable to lose them. A chase occurred. They turned quickly and spun out, and we left them in the dust. Our car broke down, my girlfriend called an old boyfriend who still pined for her, and he came and fixed the car. We snuck into my house, forty minutes late past my strict Catholic Mexican-American curfew and slid into our sleeping bags on the living room floor. "Dear God, thank you for not letting Mom and Dad find out. I promise I will ..." and I went on to dedicate the next ten years of my life to more things than Martin Luther King or Mother Teresa could have accomplished in their lifetimes.

Without moving or breathing, my left eye was twitching. I stared hard without blinking at the suspicious stars. They did move, gyrate, and come toward me. The other objects mentioned earlier go horizontal or diagonal or some such direction across the sky. They do not twirl and move straight toward the earth.

Involuntarily, I said out loud, "You are not invited here. Don't even think about it. Leave me alone, I am protected, don't even think about it. You do not have permission to show me anything at all. Especially not tonight of all nights."

Well, I'd drawn the line to the Universe or whatever. I stared, kept staring, and now three more spots of light were moving straight in. I closed my eyes for a moment to help myself calm down. As soon as I did that, I kicked myself because now I'd have to reopen them, and what would be there?

I counted up to three, figuring I'd open my eyes then. It took three times of counting to three. I opened my eyes and involuntary steeled myself for whatever would be there. Nothing was there; no more moving lights in the whole sky. All was quiet, calm, and peaceful. If it were possible, even the muted colors on the mountains were softer and more beautiful, their jagged edges seeming less jagged. I was too wound up, okay, freaked out, to be relieved.

My nerves were stretched tighter than the belly of a nine-and-a-half-months-pregnant woman. I had disciplined myself since my early years that if you want something, you set a goal and you go get it, whatever it takes. My goal was to spend the night at Machu Picchu and face my fears. My nerves may have been stretched to their limit but a core decision within myself had been set in motion. I would not "break," so to speak.

Funny how our mind adapts. Stretched like a rubber band,

irretractable goal set in motion, what's a Leo with Capricorn rising to do? Register the sensation and experience the last ten minutes in the most objective way possible. My mind immediately reverted into "check off list" mode.

Alright, twinkling lights coming toward me, completely unnatural trajectory, the absolutely clear sky, no alcohol or drugs taken previously by observer, nerves and brain ricocheting within a bag of skin and bone, DefCon 3 alert … Close eyes, open eyes. Alright, been there, done that. Move on, simple. Maybe that's the mindset that a warrior has to take in battle. That "shut down yet never more alert" state. I am in no way comparing myself to that noble professional of the highest levels of warriorhood. I am only saying that in those moments of great fear, I was able to, if only for a few moments, go into "check off list" mode.

Closing my eyes, I moved my head so it was no longer in the position of sky-watching. My head was looking straight ahead. On the count of three (which I had to do three times), I quickly opened my eyes and looked straight ahead to the deep purple mountainsides in front of me. The top of my head felt prickly as I raised my eyebrows and, ever so slowly, my head, ever so gingerly, skyward. Normal, absolutely normal. The exquisite cobalt blue blanket twinkled quietly and calmly. My head gyrated around as I thoroughly checked out every corner and inch of that mysterious blue yonder. With no clouds overhead and the full moon yet to rise, it became clear to me.

I was under a beautiful night sky and that was it. I still am not sure to this day if I was more relieved or irritated. I sat down for a moment to regroup. That sky drama had pulled the plug on my energy and I felt like a used, wrung-out dishrag. It is amazing how we allow our Fear Vampire to have a full-course buffet whenever it wants. My Fear Vampire had just wreaked havoc like a bunch of teenage boys at an all-you-can-eat Italian Tex-Mex Sunday Brunch at the Marriott Hotel. The Fear Vampire was satiated, at least for the time being. I was completely wiped out as a result.

Suddenly, I was very weary and wanted to find the "right" place to spend the rest of the night. Just in case I fell asleep, I wanted it to be a place that I perceived as well-protected, although I didn't quite formulate being well-protected from what or who as a deliberate thought. I found myself moving toward the Temple of the Sun.

I began thinking of Toby and the incredible experience he had had at the Temple of the Sun at night a few years previously. Of course, where else to be the night before the Solstice than the Temple of the Sun? Or could it be that my inherent competitiveness wanted to "beat" Toby out of who had the best experience there?

The Temple of the Sun. A most significant yet small temple located on the west side of Machu Picchu. To even get a glimpse of comprehension as to what the Inca and pre-Inca peoples felt about the Sun is difficult, if not impossible, for people of today. To most, the Sun is merely to see without assistance during the day when one comes out of whatever size cubicle one spends the day in. To all ancient peoples, the Sun meant the sustaining and growth and stimulation of "life" in all its aspects.

South of the equator, the seasons are reversed from that of the North. The June Solstice is in Peru's winter. June Solstice marks the shortest day of the year. For the ancient Incas, this special day celebrates the light of the Sun once more returning to Pachamama, Mother Earth, and all the powerful symbols of fertility, life, and regeneration that it would imply. From that day onward, Father Sun, Intitaytanchi in the native Inca language of Quechua, blesses the earth in ever-lengthening caresses with Pachamama.

I made my way to the Temple of the Sun by starlight along the narrow corridors with high, perfectly cut original Inca stone walls. I looked straight ahead as I snaked my way through the stone labyrinth.

The five ceremonial steps lay like slabs of white chalk in front of me as I turned the last corner. The flimsy wooden gate to block out tourists from entering this sacred place and altar lay across the top. Without skipping a beat, I ascended the steps, put my leg over the top of the gate, hauled myself and my stuff over, and stood there, heart pounding. The perfectly curved beautiful outer wall of the Sun Temple filled my entire visual field. The solitary doorway inside was just out of my sight. I had come here drawn to the significance of the Sun Temple on the eve of the Solstice for my "Big Experience." I did not put it together at the time that this was also one of the rare places in Machu Picchu that one had to deliberately go out of one's way to get to. Only one doorway, only one entrance, perched above another temple. In other words, it could be my bunker.

This was not in my mind, however. I was hoping for a glimpse into the mysteries of the ancient Crystal City here in the higher dimensions. I thought that by asking for all my fears to be revealed thus being freed from them, I would have permission to enter it. I would have proven I was worthy. This made sense that if I was going to have a peak experience, it would happen here! I stood riveted at the top of the stairs, realizing that I'd been almost holding my breath as I navigated the corridor and came up the stairs. I waited a few moments so my breathing and heart rate could stop disturbing the silence of the place.

The individually curved stones of the Sun Temple's exterior wall, interlocked in perfection, calmly just stood there. The pressure of a heavy brick seemed to press on the top of my head as it dawned on me that I was afraid to walk up and turn into the doorway. I did not look back or glance back down the stairs. I had to go through that doorway.

The seven steps it took to cover the ground from the top of the steps to the entrance were like walking through mush. I stood in the doorway and there it was, my goal for the night. The huge slab of stone that was the Sun Temple ceremonial altar.

The natural stone altar just about takes up the entire enclosed space and raises up about three feet. There are three windows: north, south, and very importantly, east. It is the east window that the first rays of the Winter Solstice morning sun stream through, directly striking this altar on its eastern point, and then shoot across the entire rock. Through the only doorway, I had entered this sacred space from the west, the direction that swallows up Intitaytanchi and his light every day. One can see the ancient people's purpose of a western entrance. The west is where the sun sets, bringing the dark of night. The direction of the West, in most ancient cultures, also symbolizes "Death," and traveling to the OtherWorld.

It was here in the Sun Temple that I'd make my bed for the night. I settled myself in on top of the altar. Not really a respectful thing to do on an altar; however, in the circumstances in which I was there, I felt it was okay. I was there for a spiritual purpose. I became aware of an ever-increasing sensation from my bladder.

"Great," I told myself. "No way can I pee in a temple." Also, I could not face walking all the way out of the labyrinth, down the long ceremonial flight of stone steps to the grassy plain in the middle of Machu Picchu that separates the living quarters on the east side from the ceremonial temples on the west side. I decided to fall back on my well-trained nurse's six-hour bladder capacity, and quit drinking water. I prayed I could last in that mode.

I lay uncomfortably on the stone altar, exhausted and achy. Even my eyelashes felt vulnerable. The llama blankets I lay on, with the other thrown over me, did not keep the cold from the stone from creeping into my bones. My face was freezing except where I put it under the llama blanket. Then I could hardly breathe. My head and feet were toasty, my scarf covered my ears and throat, my polypropylene pants and two pairs of long johns, my three llama sweaters, two T-shirts, and polypropylene underwear topped off by my cherry red Australian sheep super deluxe wool cape. It was weird. So warm, yet the cold reverberated to and from my bones. I thought to myself, "Well, you have all these warm clothes on so that's good." I waited for some level of comfort to tap in. It never came.

Minutes must have gone by. I became acutely aware of all the minutest points in the rock digging into my skin. My body wanted to sleep badly but I knew I had to stay awake as part of this experiment and initiation with fear. To paraphrase a War of Independence leader, Israel Putnam at the Battle of Bunker Hill, "Look at it until you see the whites of its eyes."

My head lay at the east window opening. I wanted to see how the alignment of the east energetically worked with my body and the Pleiades constellation that was aligned with that window. Maybe some comfort would come from this.

The Great Builders of the site were unparalleled in understanding astronomy and mathematics. The entire ancient site of Machu Picchu is a testament to that. These three windows were aligned to three constellations that obviously had great significance for the people, yet the details are not known as to why they were significant. The east window was for the Pleiades, the south window the Southern Cross.

We choose that which we fear. With my head on this cold slab, I asked myself, "You're lying east to west, for what? A while ago, you almost screamed out of fear that you were not open to any shenanigans from the sky. And now you lie here hoping to maybe get a glimpse of Toby's incredible experience of the connection up to the Pleiades." I figured that in this sacred site, only "good" uplifting experiences would be programmed around this stone anchor of the light of the Sun. The de-crescendoing of my anxiety to a quieter hum was a relief. Above me the stars twinkled. Through the window portals were the constellations. Now I could wait for my "big wow" on this pad leading to the light.

Suddenly, a huge beam of light from directly across the mountain came shining into the window. My first thought was how the heck could headlights be way up there. That would have to be what was making that huge of a beam. However, the light covered too broad an area, so headlights as a source had to be eliminated immediately.

I stared and waited. One minute, there was diffuse but bright white light. The next minute (or whatever time, as time had no context of meaning for me at that point), a gigantic, bright silver full moon began popping out like a jack-in-the-box in slow motion. I sat up and stared, unblinking, hardly breathing and not wanting to miss the majesty of this so exquisite beautiful moment.

How special to be lying there alone in this Power Place® on the Solstice Eve. The opening that frames Father Sun returning for his Royal Union with Pachamama. And to my delicious surprise, the full moon hung from a slice of heaven right over my head.

Sun, Moon, and Stars all converged on my head. New Agers would have one interpretation, astrologers would have another, and astronomers would have their perspective of "Interesting heavenly body lineup." Catholics wouldn't care, a Jewish mom would ask, "And what good did it do you?" My mom would be happy because it made me happy, and most everyone else would say, "Who cares and what's the point?"

All was silent as the backlit silver disc continued its steady, slow rise over the jagged mountain peaks. It was as if all creation in this slice of the universe was pausing to admire and fully appreciate the spectacular entrance of the Great Lady. Then she just hung there, free in the black cobalt sky, her presence now completely unfurled in all its gorgeousness.

My lids became heavy, and I was beginning to feel less tense after the incredible display of the Silver Mistress. I placed my head west, on the other side of the slab, to check the energetics. To my relief, the rock altar was a bit more comfortable in this direction, or was it that I was finally beginning to not be so afraid? I settled in to stare at the stars and wait for the Silver Mistress to continue her arcing slow dance over the heavens.

Lying there, I started doubting myself and wondering if this was going to turn out to be a complete dud. I couldn't feel anything emanating from this slab. Wasn't I good enough to feel something here? When I'd visited before, it was very potent. Why was it completely a zero on this night, when I had my full body draped across it for who knows how long? How many more hours until daylight? For how many more hours must I lie here? No doubt about it, I was getting antsy, and I didn't know why.

I don't know how much time passed when I sensed, before I heard, the fateful shuffling noise. That's the only way to describe it. At first it was very, very faint and far away. My brain's automatic reaction was for me to turn on my right side and mentally refuse even to register the sound. In the beginning moments, it was far enough away that this ploy worked. The steady shuffling became a little louder with each passing moment. My left ear kept registering the sound that was now unmistakable … It was a deliberate steady shuffling, of multiple feet, becoming a bit louder in each passing moment. I just lay there, like the stone altar I was on. What had been a faint diffuse shuffle now became clearer. No doubt, this was six feet, very close together, shuffling in synchronistic steps.

I was covered in boils of fear. That added to the increasing discomfort of the altar from each tiny stony projection, which took on the form of little demons poking more fear into me. My mind raced to logically evaluate the facts:

1) Synchronized shuffling is caused by "someone" alive. 2) This sound was being caused by more than one someone. 3) People would have to come over the mountain pass from the Gateway of the Sun, down the side of the mountain, which is a tiny trail. Even in the full moonlight, this would be extremely difficult and dangerous. 4) People in the site unbeknownst to me were moving around. Why would they be moving in so deliberate and nonstop a fashion as this shuffling? It was quite a labyrinth to get to where I was. At a certain point in the corridor, it leads only to where I was.

With skin demons crawling over me, prickling my skin and

having a field day, I suddenly experienced, for the first time in my life, the phrase "breaking out in a cold sweat." Dripping wet under two llama blankets, still on my right side, I thought I would go deaf from my heart pounding! The shuffling became much louder.

The shuffling was now in the part of the corridor where it could only lead to one place, this altar. On my right side, I was facing away from the doorway. I could not move, paralyzed. I had become one giant ear. As if expanding my auditory capability so more information would come to my neurons would bring a totally different conclusion than to what was looking undeniable in the moment. The shuffling of six feet was a short distance away. I could pick out each individual foot shuffle pattern now. I was a Gigantic Ear!

Louder, louder, shuffling mixed with my heart clanging like a five-alarm fire bell, me as a Gigantic Ear, dripping sweat. The shuffling was at the doorway, it was my whole existence. The huge presence of a hand shook my left shoulder savagely. My whole body shook. I was in slow motion as the shaking caused me to turn. I was as paralyzed as a mouse in the jaws of the cat.

I turned to see … nothing. Absolutely nothing. I don't know if I was more freaked out because there was nothing there, compared to if something had been there! I don't know how long I lay there. Long enough for the Gigantic Ear to disappear, and my breathing to become normal. I took off the T-shirts that were now soaked with sweat, so that I would quit shivering. I took a pee right outside the doorway. I had to do it. It was such a relief.

The rest of the night passed uneventfully. I met Walter and my group at the designated location for the sunrise ceremony. Intitaytanchi rose over his exact spot in the mountain, unfurling a beautiful rainbow blinding light, hitting my forehead first. "Hello, Father Sun." I guess I did look at it until I "saw the whites of its eyes."

My Life in the Great Pyramid

For years, I had wanted to spend the night in the Great Pyramid. Tonight it was finally going to happen. I had been inside so many times over the more than twenty years of bringing groups to Egypt. There were special private entrances planned for our groups during the times the Great Pyramid was closed to the public. In the old days, Toby knew the guard from a local village who was the "Keeper of the Keys" to the Great Pyramid. Toby also was friendly with the guard who was in charge of the all-important metal gate at the entrance of this greatest of Power Places®. For years, Toby went to Egypt many times a year with his transformational tour groups. He would arrange the special times directly with those two important gentlemen in their "office" next to the Great Pyramid, sitting on a camel rug and drinking some shai (Egyptian tea).

In later years, the government became stricter with the private entrances. They began to require special permission through the office of Antiquities of the Giza Plateau. Toby would obtain the private permission for our groups to be inside for two hours when it was closed to the general public. (In the old days, it was longer!)

One year, we had organized a large conference with over 270 people from twenty-one countries. We broke into small groups for the special entrance. As I accompanied each group, that week I counted eighteen hours that I had been inside the Great Pyramid in six days.

Due to my professional responsibilities I had been unable to do what I considered "proper preparation" prior to my special visit. To me, that meant quiet, solitude, fasting, meditation, and drinking lots of water. It was a concentrated effort with awareness to prepare for a special initiation.

It was finally happening. It was time for me to be inside alone in the Great Pyramid, completely in the dark. Not all night, but three hours absolutely alone.

There I stood, at the entrance to the Pyramid. It is always such a joy, the beautiful walk up to the entrance across the expansive sand, the desert on the west for thousands of miles. I was mindful of the fact that I was simultaneously excited, cautious, and expectant, of what I do not know.

I had learned a great lesson the entire night I spent all alone at Machu Picchu, the Power Place® of the Crystal City. I wasn't about to repeat that painful lesson. In a misguided attempt to be released from the anxiety in the uncertainties of life, I had mistakenly requested that I be released from "all that I fear" in one fell swoop. "What you ask for, you will receive," the old saying goes. Well, that is exactly what happened the entire night. Groups of footsteps shuffling down the corridor to the Temple of the Sun where I lay, being shaken awake by someone or something that turned out not to be there ... the longest night of my life, and scared to death the whole time.

That night at the Great Pyramid, standing at the entrance of this most wondrous of mystical monuments, I was feeling humble. I silently meditated for an experience that would reveal the sacred mysteries still present in this holy place. My mindset was respectful, receptive, conscious, prepared, grateful ... naked in heart and mind.

In most ways it began as all the other times I'd entered. At the entrance warm air from inside the Pyramid greeted me as I walked through the wrought iron gate which separates the mundane world from the world of hidden mysteries inside. The guards standing there saluted me in greeting. I asked them to turn off the lights the entire time I was inside. I heard the scraping of their sandals on the rocky floor and the soft shuffling of their galabeyas as they settled themselves down just outside the gate at the entrance for the next three hours. The metal gate at the entrance clanged shut behind me.

A final muffled sound of voices, and bam! The complete and utter plunge into darkness was as sudden as it always is. I am continually surprised and in awe at how dark "pitch black" really is! Literally, unable to see my finger in front of my nose. Soundlessly, I very slowly walked down the middle of the large tunnel carved out of the walls of Pyramid stone that make up the level passageway to the first shaft. "Alright pilgrim," I thought to myself, "now what?"

All I knew was that I was going to what is known as the "Pit" first, and then gradually make my way up by way of the shafts to the King's Chamber. I felt the old familiar internal pressure on myself start to build that this had to be "perfect." Finally, after all these years, I was here alone, a dream come true. And what would make it perfect? I did not have a clue.

I was alert, comfortable, focused yet on edge, and a touch anxious in this primordial black of blacks. My first order of the moment was to confirm I was 100 percent oriented to where I was. I knew the number of steps to the first turn and what the walls felt like from the hundreds of times I'd been in before with just a flashlight or with the decades old fluorescent light panels on, precariously hanging from the ceiling. I knew exactly where the handrails began and stopped at each section of the shafts, the curves in the stone, and how to navigate the shafts. I was aware of where there were holes in the floor to sidestep, and where the shafts narrowed and the ceiling became low. I knew how far each corner in each of the three chambers went, and I knew exactly where each corridor went. I knew how many steps made up each shaft, and where in each of the shaft walls were steel rungs I'd have to go up. I knew where the solar disc was carved into the huge red granite blocks from Aswan in the roof of the antechamber right before you enter the King's Chamber. I was ready.

I knew I felt humbled by what was about to take place. I cleared my mind so the sense of this sacred place could be revealed. I wanted to be open, non-judgmental, and without expectations. My deepest heart's desire was to have a "good" experience, whatever that meant. In millennia past, initiates had months, and even years of intense training and rigorous learning before entering into a moment that I was so privileged to be in now. Training and learning that I hadn't rigorously accomplished, and yet here I stood.

The multiple decisions I'd made throughout my life, from miniscule to gigantic, responses from the affirmative to negative, and mundane day-to-day life, had brought me to this extraordinary moment. Who did I think I was, standing here alone in the dark, in this most mysterious of places located smack in the middle of the largest land mass on earth?

I've been in there so many times it was like being in my neighborhood. It was very comfortable. I had a familiarity with this physical setup, where most everyone else had the privilege to come in but just once. Everything was so familiar about the rough-hewn stone walls, ceiling, and floor. What was different was that I was going in alone, and I was in complete darkness.

Why was I here? For what purpose, for what point? Certainly for the adventure. To look back on my life knowing that I spent three hours alone in the Great Pyramid would be satisfying. More important, I was also looking for something that was meaningful, something unexpected, something wonderful. I was looking to have a peek at, or be able to catch a few moments of other aspects of existence.

Honestly? I was looking to somehow touch the face of the Father/Mother, my soul.

In the darkness of this sacred space, I had a sudden revelation. In here existed the "mysteries of the universe." And importantly, the answers to those mysteries. And within that universe was the entrance to all universes with the answers to all mysteries. In this darkness, with this experience, perhaps I would be allowed a peek.

My greatest obstacle would be getting in the way of myself, like I have done so many times previously. Doesn't that always happen? We are reaching for something that will catapult us closer to inner peace, security, and contentment, and we sabotage ourselves.

A few minutes after the lights went off, a million questions, incessant mind chatter, and a wave of insecurity flooded over me.

It was as if the physical light switch being turned off was a loud and clear signal for my insecurity and silly mind chatter to be turned on. "What if I go to the wrong place first? 'Wrong' as far as what? What if I stay too long in one place, making my time in another chamber too short for whatever is supposed to happen there not be able to happen? What if I fall asleep during a meditation because of the profound silence, missing who knows what? But if I don't still myself, get centered, and be quiet, how is the 'face of God' supposed to get close?" And the ultimate …"If I become too still, will I fall asleep, wake up to the lights being turned on and miss everything?"

I stood there in the opening tunnel, paralyzed with the thought of making a mistake and blowing my probable once-in-a-lifetime alone time in the Great Pyramid. I then remembered something Toby had said years ago when we first began going to Egypt in the early eighties. That the Great Pyramid was a "transducer" of energy. Whatever state of awareness, mindset, or emotion is being held or experienced by the person entering the Great Pyramid, that state will be greatly magnified. The memory of his wise words brought me back to the state of calm openness that I experienced on the walk up to the Pyramid.

I would take one step at a time. Literally "one step at a time," quite gingerly throughout the next three hours. I decided to spontaneously do this life deed in my bare feet. My white galabeya swished in the profound quiet as I slipped out of my sandals. Not only was it pitch black, but I was also barefoot now. Even though I knew there were many rough steps and points in this structure where I could hurt my feet, I wanted direct contact with the floor.

For years, I had enjoyed walking barefoot through Egypt's

ancient temples. My feet were as sponges soaking up what once was and what still was. In my flowing galabeya and bare feet, I loved the sensation of the cold, hard stone underneath. Off by myself in the few moments I could catch alone away from the group, I would spread my toes, the sand as soft as talc powder oozing between each toe, which for some reason always felt so delicious. My bare feet and each toe seemed to serve as Geiger counters for the subtle energies. From one spot to the next in the temples, I'd pad around, my protruding light brown Geiger counters searching for the hidden treasure of pockets of high frequency energy. Subtle energies that could be accessed if one approached them with awareness.

So now my "Geiger counters" were on full alert as I stood at the end of the entrance tunnel. Would I go down to the Pit or head up to the Queen's or King's Chambers above? Where did my "destiny" lie first? I took the "low road" to the Pit without hesitation. By this time, all my senses were highly tuned into being in the dark. The only sounds were my thoughts, my breathing, and my hands and feet finding familiar landmarks every inch of the way. I turned left and proceeded down the four relatively short and one long stone steps, bent over, arriving at the corridor I knew would be there.

It was interesting that this corridor had an opening that ended up on the north side of the Pyramid, the original entrance. That corridor went straight down to what is known as the "Pit." Hunched over, I glanced up looking behind me. Through the small rectangular opening far away, a single star in a patch of clear night sky was visible. It was so beautiful that for a moment I was distracted by the sense of the hugeness of the universe encapsulated through that tiny opening. I turned, took a deep breath and started down the shaft face forward, head down.

After the first step, I realized I'd have to forget my usual system of going down shafts facing forward. It hurt too much being barefoot. Decades ago, the floors of the shafts were modified to accommodate masses of people moving up and down them. Planks of wood were placed on top of the stone bottoms of the shafts. These one-and-a-half by three- foot wooden planks had a strip of metal on the outer edge to prevent the wood on the edge from wearing down. The planks were at regular intervals to provide tiny "steps," secure places so the feet wouldn't slip. The problem for me being barefoot was these metal pieces were digging into the back of my toes and killing the balls of my feet. No way were my feet going to be able to stand that pressure. Turning around, I started going down backward. So now I was in the deep darkness, going down a shaft backward.

I suddenly felt much more vulnerable. I responded to that sense of vulnerability like I usually respond to feeling vulnerable in my life. I deny it, ignore it, pretend it's not there, disconnect from it. I make myself feel strong. I get stubborn because I hate that feeling of vulnerability, true even when I was a little kid.

In their new position, my feet found a way to navigate the steel strips without getting tortured. Slowly I made my way. I was more "my feet" at this moment than anything else. I no longer heard my breathing, my hands, or my thoughts—I was 100 percent feet. I would not allow thoughts of what if I slipped and tumbled all the way down or the myriad of ways I could possibly scream and no one would hear me.

Now secure and focused, I was filled with a quiet sense of excitement knowing this would be one of the best adventures of my life!

The feet quickly got into the rhythm of hugging the steel slates, then kissing off. My hands were holding onto the rails that were present on both sides. The way down seemed to stretch on and on. It was an interesting sensation that when you are in soundless pitch black, there is no sense of the closeness of your destination, no reference to distance. I just kept going down and down.

I was so into the rhythm of going down that when my left foot suddenly hit flat stone instead of another slate, it was a bit of a shock. There was a gaping hole in the wall where the wall and handrail had been. I knew exactly where I was: in the short vertical shaft leading to the doorway of the Pit. I crouched and turned around to "frog hobble," being careful not to bump my head on the very low ceiling, as I navigated the last few steps to the entrance.

I was at the entrance. I knew it before my feet and hands felt the edges of the rectangular opening. The huge gaping openness of the doorway stopped me dead in my tracks. To say my heart was pounding faster than a team of horses leading a runaway coach was an understatement.

I was not out of breath or tired from the journey down. It was fear that made my heart pound, not really wanting to step down into that pitch black space of a room. I slowed my breathing and willed my heart to slow. I walked in. Ever so slowly, I took the ten steps to the huge hole I knew was on the left side of the room. The fifteen-foot diameter hole was dug decades ago for excavation. In those ten steps, I decided that I was going to climb over the railing and straight down until I reached the bottom and then just sit there. I'd always wanted to do that, but either I never had the time alone down there or members of my group were present, and so I never did.

My hands touched the warm railing. I say warm because there are so many people in the Great Pyramid during the day, that year-round the temperature inside stays warm.

With my hands on the railing, I suddenly felt the seemingly infinite distance that hole went down. In my mind's eye, I felt if I went in, I would free-fall down and down, an "endless" sensation. Something like Alice down the rabbit hole. My intuition matter-of-factly said, "No."

Ever so gently, I stepped back from the hole a few feet and sat down on the floor. I found it fascinating that the physical sensation of blinking, closing one's eyes and feeling the heaviness of the eyelids and lashes on one's face, and having your eyes wide open yet unable to orient oneself visually, seems to cause something to click off in the brain. Something else entirely different then clicks on. I quickly made a mental note to later research the science behind this phenomena.

So here I sat, immersed in the "Sound of Silence." Our dear friend Emil, a highly regarded Egyptologist, used this term in referring to the unique energies of absolute stillness experienced in a sacred site such as in one of the tombs in the Valley of the Kings on the Nile.

I sat immobile. Sat, and waited, and waited. Nothing. What was the gift of this place? Why was I judging this experience as not "good" enough? It was very subtle, not at all like the incredible happening when I lay in the sarcophagus years back.

Twenty years ago I was inside the King's Chamber with Toby and only a couple of other people when I first had the opportunity to lie inside the sarcophagus. I had no expectations. I remember feeling pretty skeptical about anything special here, but kept an open mind.

I continued recalling my sarcophagus experience from the past. The entrance to the King's Chamber is north, and the sarcophagus lies north to south in the west end of the King's chamber. I laid my head down for the first time in the sarcophagus pointing north. I felt myself "rushing" out of myself. It is difficult to explain. Rising up, I felt myself floating and could see a silver cord that was attached to my other self. Streaks of light streamed within the dark passage the other "myself" was in.

I noticed I was lying on a bed of papyrus stalks. How I knew that these were stalks of papyrus is not clear as they were under me. It just was, and it seemed to be important to the event. A huge cobra head with a triangle above it presented itself not too far from my face. All my attention was on the cobra's hood spreading out, and its two glowing reddish-gold eyes.

I kept my eyes focused on its eyes. I knew that if I did not blink, I would "pass" (whatever that meant). I "passed," I did not blink. The body of the cobra then became really long, like what you see in the tombs with hieroglyphs of an undulating snake. The snake body was aligned with mine. Suddenly, there was a flash of violet light that gently exploded in my mind's eye and head simultaneously, and also affected my hearing at the same time. My ears now clicked into this low-pitched hum, surrounding me.

As the violet light faded, I noticed I had a red stone in my open left palm, and a yellow stone in my right palm. My hands felt warm, and the stones seemed to almost breathe, which makes absolutely no sense. On my belly button lay a red stone, although larger than my belly button. How could I see all this if I was lying down? The red stone on my belly button seemed to switch something "on" in my lower back. I felt sort of "lopsided," off balance, my right side seeming so much heavier than my left side. The yellow stone was an amber. I remember looking down on it without lifting my head or bringing my right hand up to my eyes (this also makes no sense).

I was shocked when the yellow stone, on its own volition, suddenly plopped into my vagina! It was round and touched my cervix. I hesitate to say that I was switched "on" at that point as I don't want to give the wrong impression. However, I now had perfect equilibrium, fully aligned in an "on" status. At complete absolute peace.

The brain of "myself" said, "This is really weird, what's next?" I became aware that Grandma Rosie seemed to be there, telling me this is what it is like to die. I thought to myself, "Gosh, why would anyone resist death?"

My mind returned to the present, in the darkness of the Pit, and I realized again that I was in this sacred space with no expectations. I began leaving the Pit, easily inching my way to the entrance. Reaching the opening to the shaft, I felt the urge to turn around. I looked over my left shoulder and my senses told me that: 1. Something was in the way-back of the Pit up the roughly hewn steps about twenty-five feet or so back to another part of the chamber. 2. No way was I going back there. 3. "Chicken," I said to myself, as I bent my head down and slowly brought both feet up and squatted neatly and with relief, back into the shaft.

Four things were happening simultaneously and I chose to "close my eyes," so to speak, in the moment of wanting to have my wits about me to carefully navigate those first few steps back out into the shaft. The first was that I was nervous and afraid of what I had sensed in the back of the chamber. Probably every childhood scary memory was coursing through every neuron in my brain at the moment. My medical background and experience had taught me to stay calm in emergencies and focus on the task at hand. Drawing on this experience, I could ignore how scared I was about "it."

Second, I was extremely unhappy with myself for not facing "it." I barely did face up to "it" in Machu Picchu, that long, lonesome, frightening night, however weakly. Third, when I had been quietly sitting there on the dusty floor of the "Pit" and my intuition said to leave, I did. Maybe I can get a bit of comfort from the fact that at least I didn't run.

Fourth, in traveling to Power Places® around the world and generally just in life, I've found that intuition and the "Divine Universal Window of Opportunity," according to the Cosmic/ Time Calendar, go hand in hand. I've learned the hard way never to ignore my intuition, no matter what. When my intuition said to leave the Pit, I did.

Now I faced the long climb up. I was calm as my bare sole hit the first metal bar across the plank. I felt in the "groove" as I methodically and mindfully made my way up the planks. I noticed a sensation of fullness in my head that became more pronounced as time passed. My medical orientation made the observation that, "Oh, this is just due to sensory deprivation," as even my footsteps became soundless. The only sound was my galabeya softly flapping with each step until I pulled it up just above my knees to silent it. When I got to the turn, I purposefully did not look up to see the square slice of night sky at the end of the shaft. That would have given me a landmark, some perspective. It would have brought in a sense of place and time. At this point, I had no idea how much time had gone by, not a clue. Time was no more.

Here I stood, exactly back where I had started at the beginning of this journey: the junction of shafts, steps, and the main exit tunnel out. I climbed the five steps up to the next shaft, a transition space leading to the entrance shaft of the Queen's Chamber and the bare-walled Grand Gallery, as it is called.

I felt comfortable going up this small enclosed "transitional" shaft; I always do. Most people rush up or down, seeing it only as a place to get somewhere else. Me, I have always liked the feeling of being tucked in there. I always stop, if I can, to savor the sense of ease and comfort. It's the safety, comfort, and nurturing of being in mother's arms before any of the disappointments or pain from life have made their disturbing presence known. I am one with the stone deep in the earth.

My hands curved around the sharp edge of the stone block and I knew I was at the end of the shaft. I was at the junction of the huge Grand Gallery and the tunnel to the Queen's Chamber. Slowly I stood, waiting for the heartbeat to slow and the breathing to quiet from the climb. It was a sign of respect to pause and gather myself together before I entered the final tunnel which led to the Queen's Chamber. Pausing before entering a holy place, a Power Place®, a place of sacredness, is important for centering your awareness in order to maximize your experience. The tunnel entrance was a place to become aware of the fact that one was leaving one world, and consciously about to enter another world.

I bent over, squatted on my haunches, placed one hand on each side of the stony shaft and started the long journey to the literal heart of the Pyramid, the Queen's Chamber. The horizontal shaft in some ways was easy traversing. By now, not having a clue on time or how much longer I'd be inside, I felt I was in a rhythm with my body. Slowly yet easily and comfortably, I waddled like a duck in my galabeya, barefoot down the tunnel. I was in tune with my senses and acutely aware of every step I took.

I became aware of a slight echo of movement. This was my cue that I must be almost at the end of the tunnel and approaching the entrance of the Queen's Chamber. I felt calmly excited and, well, happy to be there! Entering with respect, I walked the few steps to the middle and stood for a moment. Taking a few deep breaths, I noticed that a sensation of peace, calmness, and a sense of support had enveloped me.

I moved to the finely marked seven-tiered crevice in the eastern wall. Sitting at the bottom of this crevice, I scooted in as far as I could. This seven-tiered crevice is the power point in the Queen's Chamber, its Holy of Holies. I lay down. My body started feeling very heavy. I had my eyes open all the time. I liked the thought of the incongruency of my eyes being open yet registering complete blackness.

I lay there thinking about this, and the fact that the air chamber shafts in this chamber were in alignment with the constellation Sirius at certain times of the year. In Egyptian mythology, some say that Isis, the goddess of medicine and healing, supposedly originated from Sirius.

The next series of sensations began so subtly that at first they didn't register. I can describe them as feeling a gentle breeze flowing in my body. It was as though my body was a tunnel, and this breeze was moving from beneath my toes and feet, through my body, up and out of my head. Then what began as a gentle swish began to escalate to a persistent, even and steady, soft, all-enveloping powerful wind. I felt the sensation of getting swept up and moving in this quiet but powerful wind tunnel. I was somehow going somewhere, simultaneously as I experienced the sensation of being separated from my body lying in the seven-tiered niche. I hardly wanted to breathe, as I did not want to interfere with whatever the heck was happening.

I'll just describe what happened next. I was a speck going through the night sky, passing too-numerous-to-count specks of light. The further I went, the faster the speed, the smaller and denser I became, the more expansive the sensation of the space beyond the sky. The dichotomy of the hugely expansive feeling paralleled being a pinpoint of light, and it was quite odd. I have no explanation of what was occurring, and I still don't. Gradually, the speck became more diffuse, the swishing wind/tunnel sensation diminished until I was aware I was completely focused on my breathing. My breathing was slow and deep. I felt an incredible calm. I was peaceful, gigantic, and yet extremely alert. My body felt rested and rejuvenated as if I had had hours of the deepest level of sleep possible. I lay perfectly still.

Slowly, deliberately, purposefully, and matter of factly, I made my way across the Queen's Chamber to the entrance and back through the shaft. I reached the end of the tunnel and turned around. I sensed a comforting wave directly emanating from the Chamber, going directly into my heart. The feeling was as when you leave a group of true loving friends and turn to wave goodbye right before you turn the corner.

I was peaceful to my bone marrow as I stood at the bottom of what is known as the Grand Gallery. Most in the modern world are completely unfamiliar with silence. I mean true silence, including the absence of the sounds of nature. This luscious, all-enveloping silence was turning out to be something that I did not even know I craved. It's hard to imagine the deep sense of relief that happens when one is free from all sound! Throughout my time so far in the Pyramid, I was doing everything in my power to be soundless, even with my barefoot steps. The deeper the silence, the more I reveled in it, feeling as if I had snuggled into this marvelous and safe, soundless womb.

At that point, I had to make the decision of which set of steel rungs I would go up to reach the main ramp of the Grand Gallery. Choosing the three rungs on the left, up I went. The rungs are tubes of smooth steel; however, they were uncomfortable to navigate as I had to put my full weight on each steel tube with a bare foot.

I took the small step-down to the main ramp and turned around to be able to walk up the ramp. The Grand Gallery is actually a gigantic space, twenty-six-feet high, and 150 feet long. It is bare walls and stripped of any carvings or symbols. To me, it always had been just a huge spacious stairway between the Queen's and King's Chambers. Its only purpose was to connect two important places, nothing terribly significant by itself. This was so wrong as I was just about to find out.

Suddenly, my brain started registering the fact that I could "see" my galabeya, my feet, my hands. They were glowing. In a reflex action, I looked up and around, thinking that the electrical lights were being turned on and my time in the Great Pyramid was over, but there remained only complete darkness. Looking at my hands and feet glowing, I took each step slowly, fascinated by my galabeya swishing as it glowed too! There was only one thing to do. Keep on walking. Whatever was happening, I did not want it to stop, so best to keep walking.

I looked to my left, and the walls of the Grand Gallery were covered in what looked like huge sheets of soft gold, shiny and reflective as any mirror. I could see myself glowing in that sheet of gold. There appeared to be a soft, reflective light coming from inside these gold sheets. I kept on staring into the gold sheets at my left as I slowly continued walking, fascinated with seeing my glowing reflection. There were a series of sheets lined up along the walls. Each sheet touching and connected to the other. It was as if there were rooms on the other side of these sheets, rooms approximately twelve by seven feet. I then looked to the right. I saw the same situation, a soft golden reflective surface, both sides lighting up as I stepped in front of that space, but dark further up and behind me.

I stopped and stared at the one on my right, and as I did, it kept repeating the scene onto itself, over and over again like when you put a mirror up to another mirror. Staring into the soft gold mirror, seeing myself glowing, aware of the soft golden mirror directly behind me, there was sudden movement in the mirror in front of me. It was more of a blur, actually. Before I could become frightened, I saw movement, another movement, which would have to be coming from behind me in order to be reflected in front of me. I stood mesmerized as to what was before me.

In a flash, the following scenes were overlaid all upon each other, each mirror with its own multiple scenario, each distinctly clear. I simultaneously saw all the scenes and felt emotions associated with each scenario, yet I was also an objective observer. A woman in her late teens was lying on her back in the shade of a huge boulder. She was surrounded on all sides by nothing but flat desert and sand, with nothing growing as far as the eye could see. I (yes, I mean I) could feel the cool scratchy sand through my clothes and on the back of my legs. She (I) looked up and saw the brightest blue sky. Then a slippery sleeping newborn baby was held up to her face so she could sniff its fragrance before it was placed on her left breast to suckle. At that exact moment, the face of a man in his thirties filled her view, and she was aware of how much love was emanating from those sky-blue eyes in the face of the dark bearded man she loved. His scent also filled her, and she was complete.

Under my feet, I felt the jostling rumbling sensations of a chariot. I saw my masculine, strong muscular arms holding with confidence the reins of a beautiful and powerful yellow golden horse. Its heart was completely mine. We were one unit. The horse inhaled, and I exhaled. Together, we had our own language. Glancing around, I saw others as we raced across the plain to the mountains in the far distance. What a young man, the epitome of freedom, strength, and the joy of being alive.

A little girl of three was happily planting tiny seeds in freshly turned-up soil. The overwhelming smell of fresh, raw earth enveloped her as she carefully placed one tiny seed after another, lovingly covering each one with the rich soil. She absolutely loved the feeling of the earth and the waves of scents as she moved the soil. She played with it, making a cave home for each seed, and then carefully placed the dirt roof back on each, gently patting each spot. She felt before she heard a horse coming her way. As her eyes swept the green grass and lush rolling hills, her heart sang when she saw who was coming toward her. It was her daddy, tall, dark, and handsome, with a dazzling smile and teeth and spar-kling blue eyes. She grabbed the remaining tiny seeds and flew to her daddy. He scooped her up in his arm, and plopped her in front of him on the muscular back of his black stocky horse. Supreme happiness was hers. Her father's arms were holding her, the strong back of the horse was underneath her, and her beloved seeds were in her sweaty little palm, protected, as was she.

The ancient crone was cold and achy sitting hunched over in the lean-to, not much protected from the elements by the thin wall of trees. She loved her herbs, grasses, mosses, flowers, and tree barks. They fueled her spirit, keeping her heart's fire lit. She enjoyed nothing more than searching the forest for ingredients whose inherent power comprised her healing concoctions. Crushing them up with an ancient stone rock, she would sing-song the exact words that would make the concoction come alive. She knew the right combinations of ingredients had been reached when the concoction sang back to her, their songs becoming one.

The scenes faded but still the golden mirrors glowed. I saw my reflections disappear, then the golden mirrors faded. I was no longer glowing. All was deep darkness and black once more.

This was part of the ancient initiations. A final major test. One could easily become enthralled here. Glowing with gold light on this riveting ride through time, fascinated by the multiple scenes of past lives on the soft gold sheets, one's ego could easily be dazzled, never making it to the ultimate initiation goal, the sarcophagus in the King's Chamber.

It was quite jarring to once again be in the absolute darkness. I missed the sensation of seeing the golden glow coming off my hands, feet and galabeya. I made my way up the gallery. I instinctively knew the end of the ramp, when to stop, when to reach out and touch the wall right in front of me. I climbed up the three steel rungs to the entrance of the antechamber of the King's Chamber.

I paused then entered after bending over at the waist, like a ceremonial bow. I took the two steps in and then could stand in the tiny space. It really wasn't a chamber but an opening in the blocks of the ceiling of the shaft. I stood up and waited there, the wall two inches in front of me. My right hand reached up to the high relief of the solar disc directly in front of me on the wall.

I was growing, not only filling this tiny space in the antechamber, I was also spreading into the solid red granite, my head going through the ceiling. I can only describe the experience as being a "living rock." The solar disc was pulsating in my right hand as my left hand dangled at my side. There was a strong yet pleasurable sensation that my toes were inhaling and exhaling, as if my toes were lungs. I remember not wanting to take any steps for fear that the wondrous sensation would disappear before I had my fill.

Bending over, I navigated the last few steps through the small tight shaft leading to the King's Chamber. Purposefully, silently, and mindfully. I was in. I stood just inside, taking a few deep breaths as I oriented myself. Quietly and reverently, I walked over to the sarcophagus, lifted my leg over the rim, dropped in, and lay down. My head was north, my feet south, my left to the east, my right to the west. I waited.

I felt myself being pulled down, down, down, at a comfortable speed. Simultaneously, I was floating up, feeling more and more expansive. An indescribable feeling of sublimely deep peace prevailed. This is what must be meant by Eternal Peace. In that moment, I knew I would never again be afraid of dying.

Given a clear and undrugged mind, a spiritual and emotional preparation for dying, the recognition and acceptance that the moment is soon to come ... the dying process must be brilliant.

Now, it is something I look forward to as the greatest adventure of my life!

In that moment, every cell 100 percent knew, experienced, and understood that the point of living life and all its joys, pains, losses, and highs was in preparation for those final inhalations and exhalations.

Each day is a death and a life. Each blink is a death and a life. Each breath is a death and a life. Every laugh is a death and a life. Each look into someone's eyes is a death and a life. Each smile is a death and a life. Each memory we think of is a death and a life. Each expression of love or caring is a death and a life. Each time we choose not to express love or caring, it is a death and a life. Each thought we have toward ourselves of belittlement, put-down, or judgment is a death and a life.

There is not a moment of being a human being in this world that we are not simultaneously living and dying, dying and living, each aspect capable of bringing incredible joy and freedom and peace.

I perceived a diffuse low yellow light through my closed eyelids. I heard the familiar low-pitched hum of the old-fashioned fluorescent light bulbs, meaning the lights had been turned on downstairs by the guards. I opened my eyes and knew from experience that in less than five minutes, the overhead electrical lights would be fully on. My time was finished. It was time to leave.

Slowly, I clambered out of the sarcophagus. I sat on the floor in the middle of the chamber and then just lay down. No doubt about it, I did not want to leave.

It was very strange indeed to go all the way down, retracing my steps through the King's Chamber, antechamber, five rungs, and the Grand Gallery. When I reached the landing at the end of the Grand Gallery, I wanted to go running, scrambling, and crawling down the tunnel to the Queen's Chamber. I wanted to throw myself on the floor there, like a child would run into its mother's full skirt and comfortably wrap the fabric and smell of Mommy all around. I did not; it was dark in there and there was no time. So I just bent down and peered into that long tunnel for a moment.

I left the Grand Gallery, turned around, and went down the middle shaft backwards. My feet were heavy as they hit the last five stone steps, leaving me at the beginning of the long tunnel to the outside. In that moment, I felt as if I'd always been in the Pyramid, had lived my entire life there, and that there was no other life or world. It was the oddest feeling, not emotional at all. It was just factual, that this was my only life.

I walked through the entrance tunnel to the gate still in this "otherworldly" state, for want of a better word. I picked up my soft beautiful golden brown abaya, a special gift from a dearest friend. Made of the finest wool, in the millennia-old traditional way. Hand-stitched by an old woman in Upper Egypt, just like the ancients. In slow motion, I placed the abaya over my shoulders, and the familiar scent, sound, and comforting feel of it falling down my shoulders and back made me acutely aware that I was leaving that place.

The muffled voices of the guards wafting up from outside the entrance of the tunnel were like a sharp slap inside my head. I did not feel ready to hear voices, or have to speak to anyone or relate to anyone. Very reluctantly, I drifted out into the night air, seeing the distant lights of Cairo and hearing the far-off muffled sound of its "city noise." The guard, whom I've known for years, asked, "Good?" I slowly smiled and whispered "Good."

Near-Death on the Nile

Surrounded by desert, smack in the middle of nowhere, Jackie was suffocating to death. Lying on a table, her knees bent, legs spread wide, I wondered, "Why does this remind me of all the women in the delivery room I've seen, and the one too many pelvic exams I've done?" The answer to that question boggles my mind to this day.

I clearly remember that narrow exam table and her legs and feet repeatedly slipping off it, shaking her body and making it impossible to start an IV. It was imperative she immediately received intravenous medication to allow her to breathe. After years of my working in the ER and ICU it was crystal clear she was already in anaphylactic shock, within minutes of dying.

Earlier that morning, our group was to experience the magnificent Temple of Horus at Edfu, about a mile from the Nile River and the cruise ship the group was on. Jackie started passing out at the entrance. Someone yelled for me, I grabbed Mohamed, and we ran to the commotion. Mohamed scooped her up just as she fainted. A taxi suddenly appeared. We hightailed it to the little clinic a few blocks away. The clinic was spotless but rudimentary.

The nurse suddenly appeared. On my questioning her where the oxygen equipment and emergency medication were, through Mohamed's interpreting, she pointed to the equipment to start an IV. However, no oxygen or IV medications or solution were evident. Unfortunately, it had been a long time since I had started an IV in a collapsed vein. I desperately needed Benadryl and/ or epinephrine to relax her bronchi, which were spasming thus squeezing the life out of Jackie by the second.

Purple face, purple tongue, black lips, mottled purple hands, the weird color creeping up her arms … eyes rolled back. Standing on her left side, I quickly went through the ER drill for checking how conscious someone is before instituting CPR. However, if the bronchi are swollen and closing, the amount of oxygen flow is minimal at best.

No response to deep painful stimuli. I knew she was going; we were losing her. She was about to die. Repeatedly, I said in as calm a voice as I could muster, "Let me know if you can hear me." The purple blackness of her extremities steadily got worse. There was no response, no movement from her.

Suddenly, I noticed a stream of wispy light going out the top of her head. It's hard to explain the rush sensation emanating from that wispy light. But I knew what the "rush" was. I knew she was about to go out to the point of no return, and die.

I yelled to Mohamed, "We're losing her! Stand at the bottom of the table and say, 'KA come back.' Get her KA back!" Of course, Mohamed had no idea what I was referring to when I instructed him to "Bring her KA back." Neither did I! I repeated, "Get her KA back." I wondered, "What am I saying? Where did that come from?"

With my will and thoughts focused, I fought to get Jackie's KA back to her body. Every bone and ounce of strength in me knew that this was not the time for her to die.

Acutely aware of her increasingly black and purple skin, it seemed like hours that I stood there in this slow motion tug of war. I felt more than saw the thread of light at the top of her head start to become thicker, reverse direction, and begin to flow back into her body. Her black purple color slowly started to disappear.

The doctor arrived with the drugs and the oxygen. We managed to start an IV and poured in the medications as fast as possible to continue reversing the anaphylactic shock and breathing difficulties.

Slowly she came to, the purple blue gone yet her face drained of color. Her eyes glazed. I continued speaking to her in a reassuring tone, repeatedly telling her she was alright. Everything was going to be fine. Then she asked to sit up on the table. "What the f___ is going on?" she managed to blurt out before throwing up.

With feet dangling and hands gripping the edge of the table, the full impact of what had just happened seemed to start to seep through her. Looking around, appearing confused yet very calm, her wide eyes conveyed the struggle to make sense of what she had just experienced.

The stark bare room of the clinic, the kindly Egyptian doctor, the helpful nurse and the IV pole dangling the plastic threads pumping the healing electrolyte saline and dextrose solution into her arm made no sense with her last memory. And that was standing outside the temple, a full-blown asthma attack gripping her, a great difficulty in breathing, members of the group coming to assistance, then feeling herself slipping away, about to die. She was thinking this, at least that is what I thought. As I was to find out later that evening, she was remembering what she had just experienced while she was dying, and it was beyond imagination.

Early in the trip, Jackie had already figured out that being exposed to all the horses and camels along the way had triggered her chronic asthma. She'd already experienced an asthma attack when we were in Cairo. Knowing of the horses at Edfu, I had mentioned to her not to go that day. Upon arrival in Edfu, I had announced that the group would be taking "caleshes" (horses and buggies) from the cruise ship to the temple site. I was going to take the morning off, however as the last person took off for the site, I suddenly changed my mind, called for a caleshe and headed for Edfu.

Why did Jackie take a horse and buggy and not a taxi, when she already knew that her recent exposure to camels and horses in Egypt was escalating her asthma to alarming levels? Why do we all make choices like that in life, when the evidence clearly points to a different path?

I can only speak for myself when I answer that for me, it is because I am avoiding the real origin of the pain. And I am avoiding it so powerfully that I will make a choice to cause "another" discomfort or pain as a distraction, whether that "distraction" be emotional, mental, or physical.

Mohamed and I helped Jackie from the table onto her feet. She swayed, unsteady as a newborn lamb. Mohamed and the doctor had a quick exchange in Arabic. I glanced at the doctor and he nodded toward a hallway. Mohamed told me there was a room with a bed where she'd be more comfortable.

We were all silent as we slowly walked down the hallway; the only sounds were our feet shuffling and the rattling of the bottles and tubes hanging on the IV pole I dragged behind her. That sound bouncing off the bare walls seemed to come crashing back at us. This surrealistic scene all seemed to take place in timeless slow motion, walking down the hallway, taking her into the small room, whispering to ask if she wished to change her soiled clothes. One moment this woman was dying, appearing to have only one toe left in this life. The next, she's walking, struggling to talk, and we are changing her galabeya to a clean one.

We took a taxi back to the ship and rode in silence. Mohamed carried Jackie into the boat and up to her room. Everyone was waiting for news on Jackie and started applauding when they saw her. Apparently, they all thought Jackie had died. Jackie's friends were waiting in her room for news, crying when they saw her and scolding her to never do that again!

Jackie immediately wanted to tell us of this most amazing experience she had when she was dying. I was thinking I already knew, and asked Jackie if she would wait to share until after I went down to the group gathering for dinner.

At dinner, I was telling everyone what had happened to Jackie that day and how she was doing, but I mistakenly kept referring to "Jackie" by the name of "Joyce." Jackie's roommates and friends huddled their heads together at their table, giving me strange looks, and whispering. I glanced over at them and could not figure out what the stir was about. When my announcement was finished, I went over and asked what was wrong. It seems I inadvertently called Jackie by her sister's name, Joyce, during the announcement. Kate, Jackie's roommate, explained to me that Joyce was Jackie's sister, and had died ten years earlier. The two sisters had been extremely close, Jackie helping raise Joyce's children after her death. I had not known about Jackie's sister, her name, nor had ever discussed Joyce with Jackie previously.

I returned to Jackie's room to check up on her after my announcements. Jackie told this amazing story: As she was trying to breath and not able to, she remembered seeing my face and my telling her not to close her eyes, to keep looking at me. She knew that she was in real trouble, she was leaving this life, and that her children were going to be mad at her since she would be coming home in a box. She now knew why it was so important to come on this trip to Egypt. She had come here to die.

Suddenly, she lost all fear of dying and just let go. Jackie could feel herself falling and then floating, no longer having trouble breathing. She felt complete "Bliss" (her quotes.) She floated into a place that looked like an outdoor temple. She lay on a long, flat stone surface, and at one point felt as if she was having contractions. I said to myself, "What? Like in labor?" Which is what Jackie looked like when she was on the table with her legs spread as she was dying.

Her friend Kate stopped Jackie right then. Kate said that after Mohamed and I took Jackie away, her friends went into the Edfu temple. There was a long, flat stone. They encircled the stone and started meditating and doing healing chantings for Jackie's recovery.

Jackie on a flat stone in a temple in her near-death experience, having labor contractions. I see her with her legs bent and spread as if she is about to deliver a child. Simultaneously, people encircling a flat stone inside the temple meditating for Jackie's recovery.

I find it incredibly fascinating that the conference/tour theme was "Life, Death, and Beyond." And that a flat stone, nothing like it seen or experienced at all the previous ancient sites, figured in both Jackie's experience and the ladies at the temple meditating for Jackie. And that Jackie's almost dying occurred next to a 2,500-year-old ancient Egyptian temple at Edfu, dedicated to the primal aspects of life, death, resurrection, and the beyond.

The Amazon:
A Healing Through Time

I was walking in the tropical rain at home. Wrapping a hand towel over my notebook and notes to prevent them from turning into sheets of pastry, I cradled the bundle in my arms as I walked up the many concrete steps from the beach. Weirdly, a flash came into my view.

Walking up a set of stone steps, a young woman (me, I realize) held a tiny bundle of lifeless flesh, my own flesh and blood. My long-awaited-for innocent newborn had been slaughtered to make a political point. I was on my way to bury my beloved son amongst the ancestors in niches high up in the Andean cliffs. My bundle of now-lifeless joy was wrapped in a heavy coarse textile but stitched with the highest workmanship. Holding my baby, walking up those stone steps, I was fifteen years old. Simultaneously, I saw myself as that girl now grown into a very old woman, going up those same fate-filled stone steps. Only this time, she held nothing. She wobbled slowly up the steps to die, to take her place amongst the ancestors. I saw that I never recovered from my baby's murder, my baby's death.

Then, I flashed to ten years ago when I was in the Amazon on a familiarization trip to research taking groups there. My accommodations were in a delightful and comfortable treetop lodge. On the way to my room, I walked the rope and wooden plank bridge in a gorgeous canopy of trees. My eye caught the sight of a light brown, white-chested little monkey, very cute, hunched over by a post at one end of the bridge.

I slowly walked over to it, bent down, and spoke gently so as not to frighten it. It turned its head toward me. I was absolutely thrilled that it let me pick it up. I turned it over to cradle it in my arms. I was shocked to see a deep diagonal gash in its chest from left to right, festering and infected.

Then something weird happened. I looked into the eyes of this young monkey, and I felt something in my heart that my brain registered as the following: This must be what a mother feels when her new baby gets placed in her arms. It was a two-way flow pouring into my heart and chest that it almost bowled me over. Interestingly, at the same time, what can only be described as a golden shaft of light came down and shone all around me. I was literally in a tube of gold, soft, glittery light. I blinked a few times, thinking maybe something was in my eyes. Or that this was merely the equatorial light playing an optical trick as it streamed through the treetops and jungle canopy, filtering the sunlight in some unknown way to me, giving the appearance of gold and glittery in a tube effect. The interesting fact is that outside the tube of glittering gold light, the light was normal. The glittery tube did not go away, and neither did the huge wave of maternal love.

I know what you're thinking. Career woman, biological clock ticking away, maternal yearnings. I have held many newborns, including my darling nieces and nephews, and I felt great love. However, not even close to what I call maternal X chromosome pull. Gently holding the wee one, I took it to my cabin. I cradled it in my left arm as I placed my right palm over his chest, sending healing energies flowing to the wound.

As a nurse, I had learned "laying on of hands" and "healing by touch" back in the mid-seventies from Dr. Toby Weiss. He and Dr. Dolores Kreiger were the only professors teaching advanced subtle energy healing techniques at the university level in those days. That little monkey just lay in my arm and closed its little eyes. I rocked it while sitting on my bed, letting the energy flow out of my hands. Eventually I closed my eyes.

Maybe almost an hour went by. I opened my eyes. The golden glittery tube of light was no longer in my visual field. I looked around. Strange how everything seemed oddly flat and two-dimensional. How was that possible in the lushness of this Garden of Eden, the Amazon? Was it my imagination that the wound was less red and not as green around the pus-filled edges? I did not feel that united connection any longer with the little monkey; we weren't one like before. Once again, we were separate human and monkey. The little monkey scampered off, chattering away. Did it have a lilt to its step now? Later on, a hotel worker told me the monkey's chest had been slashed by an alligator.

How can one explain something that has no words? What did this little monkey in the Amazon have to do with anything? Does this experience with the monkey have anything to do with my experience in Palenque two years before? I had been in Palenque in the Yucatan jungle in Mexico. Palenque was an important ceremonial, cultural, and religious site to the ancient Maya. To this day, the archeological site there has beautiful, exquisite ruins where the energies remain very powerful.

Leading a tour with a group of pilgrims one afternoon, I was just sitting there in the grass. I had a few minutes alone and I was enjoying the solitude and peace and the visual lushness of this place of antiquity. I felt comfortable and at home here, the energy wrapping around me like a wonderful, broken-in, old heavy linen cape.

Then over the next few minutes, my eyes open the entire time, a scene filled my surroundings. I first heard horrible screams and wails, horses' hooves pounding, and lots of commotion, and my nose filled with dust. Then there I was, or this young woman was, in a huge throng of masses of people, all pushing and screaming and in complete panic, trying to escape the horsemen gone berserk with their spears that were everywhere. I realized that in the pandemonium, there were no men at all, only women and children.

The horsemen were systematically killing and slashing all children and infants, but not the women. I, or rather the young woman, turned, and in her face was the flank of a huge brown-black horse. This wall of firm flesh was the entire universe in that one fateful moment. I then noticed she (as me) was cradling and protecting a bundle. I looked down, and at the exact same moment that I was just about to look deeply into the black-brown eyes of my baby son in that life, a huge metal spear appeared from above and slashed across its' chest, left to right. The newborn's blood spurted; the infant never squeaked a sound. I howled, I wailed, or I should say this black-haired, pretty-faced young woman with the most beautiful clear skin I'd even seen, howled and wailed.

It was clear that for the rest of her life, this woman never got over losing this baby. In this war, she had just recently lost her husband, the love of her life, and this one and only child had been conceived out of that joyous union. Now she had neither. She was now only a ghostly presence that was living and breathing until she was very old.

The sounds of the massacre and horses faded, and I noticed that my chest and heart were in pain extremis. There I sat in Palenque, seven years ago, my eyes still open but everything normal and peaceful. The green lush grass was soft, the jungle sounds ever present. Flash forward to two years later, in the Amazon. The monkey had the exact wound, same angle. Flash forward five years later, when I was walking up the concrete steps, and remembered that I had completely forgotten about both these strange and unexplainable yet somehow connected episodes. Why the remembering now? I confess I have not yet figured that out.

ATULA

It was the most precious of times ... the moment between the two worlds. The sun set forty-five minutes prior, the sky on the horizon was still robin-egg blue, the far clouds in the distance were a milky blue haze of shapes. The symphony of frogs and crickets had started, the tropical breeze was soft and gentle, and the waves were only whispering at the time. It had always been so easy for me to be quiet inside myself at this time of the day. If I must speak, I would wish it was only in a whisper. In this stillness ...

I saw and then I was a little girl of around six. She was kneeling back on her haunches at the head of a very old man with pure white long hair, who was lying on the ground. She was at his right ear. At first, it appeared as though he was dead. They were in a cave bathed in soft light, like candlelight. I assumed it was a candle, but it was not. Something was making the soft glow, but I do not know what it was.

He was dying. Into his ear, she was making certain sounds, whispering a string of words. She was making the sounds to help him leave his body. He was her great-grandfather, her "ATULA." For years, he had trained and prepared her for this time when she would help him die to go to the OtherSide. This was that time.

They left their village days ago and came to this hidden cave, the Cave of the Way. They were alone and isolated, no food or water. He was a great, well-respected medicine man, a wise one, the Elder and a seer (see-er) to the other worlds. If he had stayed in the village to die, the love and grief of the people would have been like chains. Their love and grief was so strong, and there were so many. He had brought his "little girl," his six year old great-granddaughter, to this cave to die after saying goodbye to all the people.

For days, hour upon hour, she bent over to his right ear, singing the words and saying the sounds exactly in the order and the way he had taught her. Steady and soft. With confidence and with love. Most importantly, with correct pronunciation. "Pronunciation is power," her great-grandfather had said repeatedly over the years. "Most ignore this simple matter. If one pronounces correctly, then one is breathing correctly. The breath controls the true destiny and power of the sounds and words."

Then, after she did not know how many days, she saw someone who looked like her great-grandfather, only many, many years younger (early thirties), come right out of her great-grandfather's body and stand behind her. She could feel his strength and energy. Her heart was full with his love for her.

As he started to walk away, she noticed he was attached with a golden cord to the figure with the long white hair lying on the floor. However, her now-young great-grandfather could not yet leave for the "OtherSide." There was one more thing to do.

How, she did not know, but she was suddenly sitting behind the right eye of this young ATULA man that looked like her great-grandfather, as he quickly went to someone in the village. He was around that person very fast, or rather, his entire presence was wrapped around this person who could not see him. In a flash, his "little girl" from behind his right eye saw everything.

This person in the village was the daughter ATULA had ignored and whom he did not take care of in his life. Her great-grandfather came back to the village to express his gratitude to this daughter. Not to ask for forgiveness, but to say thank you to her for being in his life. He could not leave for the "OtherWorld" until his daughter could feel his thoughts in her heart. The little girl sitting behind the right eye of the young man saw the daughter woman, who was older than the young man, suddenly start to cry and be happy at the same time.

NOW her great-grandfather could go. The little girl suddenly could not see and it felt as if she had a blindfold on. She held the right hand of her great-grandfather (still looking young) as they started walking in a tunnel. Even though sounds were muffled and she could not see, somehow, she already knew the way and wasn't frightened. She began hearing many strange but beautiful sounds.

Her young-looking great-grandfather stopped, turned to her, and touched her face. He put his hands to the top of her head, touched her ears, the bottom of her neck, the top of her breast-bone, and tapped her shoulders twice. There was a bright light all around, and she could barely see his face through the "not there" blindfold. He said "Kuh-HAH" and was gone.

Instantaneously she was back in the cave. Simultaneously, every inch of her body, all the way to her bone marrow, screamed in the worst deep pain that was beyond her to ever imagine. Her eyes hurt from so much desperate crying, her throat was so sore and closed, her chest was too tight for her to breathe. She thought she would strangle.

She forced herself to get up. First staggering, then somehow she started to run. She was a little girl of five. All she wanted to do was bury herself in the arms of her mother. She did not know how she had the strength to run through the dense forest and over the hill, but before she knew it, and in spite of the pain, she was at her village. She just collapsed to the ground as soon as she entered her lodge.

The next few days were a fog and haze to her. People's faces, their eyes shining with tears, came in and out of view. Always she could feel the special touch of her mother's hand. The little girl was on fire, as if a volcano was exploding inside. At the same time, she was freezing. The weight of all the furs on top made it impossible to even turn on her side.

She was only a little girl. She did not know what was happening, and could not understand. All she knew was that her whole life, her great-grandfather had always been there and was as much a part of her as breathing. Now, she couldn't "feel him" at all!

He had told her that when the time came for her to "sing the songs" for him, that this would be the most important thing anyone had done for him his entire life. She had been so proud to be with him, singing the songs and praying the words she had been practicing with him for as long as she could remember.

He had explained to her that when it came time to actually perform the ceremony with the beautiful words, songs, and sounds, she would know she had done it perfectly ... because she wouldn't feel him after that ceremony. At the time, his words to her, that she wouldn't be able to sense him, or be calmed by his scent, or see him with the one thousand eyes of her skin, were incomprehensible. "I will be with her in a different way," he had said. Her five-year-old brain did not understand at the time what he had meant. He was her great-grandfather, her "ATULA," and he was just always there, permeating her life.

As she lay with burning fever and cold, in pain, out of her mind, she still did not understand. She only knew one thing. The ceremony must have been perfect, for she couldn't feel him, smell him, touch him, or hear him. She couldn't sense him *at all*. It was as if he never had even existed.

Her mind felt happy because she knew that he was happy. But had no understanding that the source of her deep pain was the trillions of cells in her body, disconnecting from his physical presence. The threads from each cell and molecule going between them were still being gently disconnected ... his from hers and hers from his. For three days and nights, she lay like a stone under the furs, burning and freezing.

ATULA had told her that after the time that she could not feel him, she would be helping him to be born into the next world. She couldn't figure out how this grown man could come out through the "cave of life" from a woman the same way she had seen babies being born. He was way too big and tall!

On the fourth day, she understood. In the next world, every-one must be giants. Great-grandfather, at his tall height in this world, would be new-baby size in the next world! This she could make sense of. She tried to tell her mother not to worry, that it was happening as great-grandfather had instructed her. Her lips couldn't make the movements. Her breath had no power. Her throat did not have the will, so she lay silent.

There came a moment through her fog when she opened her eyes and knew what she must do. Slowly she got up, her head and mind so clear and strong. Yet her body and legs were unsteady and shaking involuntarily like a newborn fawn. She snuck out of the lodge with great difficulty. She very slowly made her way to the sacred place where she and great-grandfather had placed all his belongings on their journey to the "Cave of the Way." By the stream, on the boulder at the foot of the mountain, was where they had placed the pack after doing a ceremony together. He had told her then, "Come here later ... you will know when, and you will know what to do."

She dragged herself back to the village with the pack. One by one, she picked up an object, her hands with a mind of their own. Her feet, with a mind of their own, took her to the person this object would be given to. The recipients each had their own reaction. Each deeply moved, some surprised, some confused, all grateful.

The confused or surprised ones approached her during this time, and one after another, shared their story with her. Their story always went, "When you gave this to me, at first I did not know why great-grandfather would want me to have this. I did not understand the connection. There came a moment later when I realized this meant he understood my struggle. The gift symbolized exactly what my issue was. I am now at peace. I never told anyone about this. How did he know?"

Buffalo, deer, birds of all types, insects, reptiles, and many two-legged (humans) from other tribes and nations came to the village for the final "Going Away" ceremony. The drumming, dancing, and singing went on for days. She sat next to the drummers, letting the sound roll around deep inside of her, getting stronger and stronger.

There came the day when she could sense and feel him again. She had never experienced such joy! In the disconnecting cell by cell and atom by atom from great-grandfather, the threads returning to her carried the entire essence of him!

She had all of great-grandfather within her now. His wisdom. His knowledge of the stars, the moon language, the earth voice, the animals, birds and fish, the insects, even how to stop the wind, speak to the clouds, and hear the words and understand the language of the thunder. How to taste a morning drop of dew with the tongue to know what the plants were singing. How to look at the rainbow in a small ball of dew, reading what the earth was saying in the moment. How to touch a tree and feel its heartbeat.

She was flooded inside for a moment with all of this. His lips seemed to be on the right ear of each of her cells. The cycle was complete. She *was* the new "ATULA.

Appendix I

The KA

The KA is the ancient Egyptian word for "double." KA is the "double" or "twin" of the physical person. The hieroglyph looks like this:

The standard explanation is that the KA's shape is a symbol of "calling." More precisely, the symbol of the KA is the gesture *"for calling to the physical body,"* the person's soul. The KA is the grounding force that anchors our body to this physical reality. Simultaneously it serves as the vessel holding the presence of our soul within our body.

The stream of wispy light I witnessed coming out the top of Jackie's head was the physical manifestation of her KA leaving her body. With her soul no longer having an anchor in this physical reality, she would be dead.

As the drawing shows, the KA is depicted with arms raised up from the sides and above the head. The elbows are positioned at ninety degrees to the shoulders, making the elbows in straight alignment with the base of the neck.

This forms a "U" shape with a straight bottom: a box with a straight bottom, two sides, and an open top. The straight bottom to symbolize a sturdy foundation. The two sides symbolize protection. An open top representing the entryway for the soul.

If one emulates exactly this pose, raising arms to ninety degrees with the shoulders, with both thumbs and fingers so depicted, there is a sense of the brain almost seeming to open up. From a physiological standpoint, the heart and upper chest areas are suddenly flooded with the liquids of the blood and lymph system: more oxygen. This brings in a sense of vitality and strength and could explain the sense of the brain opening up.

After a thirty-year span of experiencing the ancient temples and tombs, one thing is undeniable. To the ancient Egyptians, there was a precise meaning or specific purpose to every dot, line, circle, curve, drawing, or color used in building their temples and tombs. Nothing was carved or put in stone without a precise definite meaning. The symbols and icons were never drawn or carved just for decoration. That all-encompassing precision is why anyone, by focusing their awareness, is able to sense the subtle energies still present today. That person may not be able to put a finger on what they are sensing; however, they will admit that there is something different there.

On that note, take a moment now to actually experience your KA.

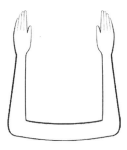

Please read the suggested steps below before implementing the steps.

Now: While sitting in a comfortable chair without arms, close your eyes and take a few deep breaths. Slowly inhale through your nose. Puckering your lips slowly exhale. (This is called purse-lipped breathing.) This type of breathing calms the nervous system bringing in an overall sense of relaxation, making it easier to focus. Breathe gently like this three times.

Next: Slowly raise your arms up from your sides, slightly above your head so your shoulders are in alignment with the base of your neck. Don't strain or put pressure anywhere.

Keep your eyes closed. Hold this position for a few moments while you continue the purse-lipped breathing.

Open your eyes. Take a few moments to internally make a note of what you may or may not be sensing inside yourself after this experience.

I wish to point out that it is important not to compare "KA" to the late nineteenth century taradiddle term "aura" that California New Agers got ahold of in the seventies, and popularized at the beginning of the hippy movement. The KA is not an aura.

I am intrigued by the KA and there remains for me many questions about it.

For instance, was my entire experience with Rose, where I first inhale and end with the final exhalation, my KA moving out of my body, and then coming back? If so, would it follow that it was my KA that went with Rose to that exquisitely beautiful meadow of gold light?

Was being "out of my body" really a KA experience?

With visions and apparitions of dead people, are we seeing their KA return? Is this what was happening when I saw Grandma Rosie at her own funeral, and Grandma Panchita and Tata at Dad's fiftieth birthday party?

What happens to the KA when the person dies? Immediately thereafter? Is there a difference when it's an accident or suicide, versus a natural-death scenario?

Do we all have our own KAs?

All intriguing questions beyond the purview of this book. However, in a future publication, I intend to share my research on this fascinating subject of the KA.

Appendix II

The Six-Pointed Star: Transport Between Worlds

I am fascinated by the two solid six-pointed stars and their signif-icance to the Deathwalk. They are the vehicles to the "OtherSide." At the beginning of the Deathwalk, the two solid stars come together. My left palm, with its six-pointed star, congruent to the six-pointed star in the middle of Grandma's forehead. This merging of stars begins the extraordinary sequence of events as we transport to that exquisite golden place of peace.

Their melding provided the potent propellant to "The Hill of Perpetual Golden Light."

What does this symbol mean? And what do the solid six-pointed stars have to do with us traveling to the next level immediately after Grandma Rosie died?

The solid six-pointed stars are tranducers, devices that convert a signal in one form of energy to a signal in another form of energy. My star's signal originated from the earthly plane of existence.

The Apex Up triangle represents "earth." The earth's life-force energies travel up from the base, concentrating at the apex, the point of power.

Grandma Rosie's star signal originated from the spiritual realm of existence.

The Apex Down triangle represents subtle energies from a higher spiritual realm being funneled down concentrating this essence in the apex.

While I am neither a mathematician nor an expert on Euclidian geometry, I am confident in sharing this description. When broken down, the solid six-pointed star is two equilateral triangles, with internal angles at sixty degrees. Lined up, apex to apex, imagine the solid triangles moving through each other until they are overlaying at each of their midpoints. This reveals the final shape of the solid six-pointed star.

In the creation of the solid six-pointed star, the point of power, the apex, of the concentrated earth energy triangle gets bisected by the apex of the spiritual realm triangle. The concentrated power of higher "essence" distilled to a single point, moves down, bisecting the base of the earth energies triangle. The merging of the energies of " heaven" and earth.

Appendix III

Recreation as Re-creation

Instead of a mundane, "didn't get away at all and you come home less than satisfied" vacation, suppose next time you take a vacation you decide to venture out on a special journey. You "vacate" your everyday life on a quest of renewal and recreation looking for a transformational trip. No place is better suited to this than one of the world's "Power Places®."

What is a "Power Place®?"

A "power place®" is a planetary center of concentrated energy. Places like the Great Pyramid of Egypt, Machu Picchu, Stonehenge in England, Mt. Everest, the Mayan pyramids, and the temples in Tibet are good examples. "Power Places®" are either man-made monuments or nature sites, or a combination of the two. Examples of nature sites would be Yosemite, the Grand Canyon, and Iguazu Falls. Many people have "peak" experiences at these places. These "peak" experiences-of-a-lifetime become building blocks in re-creating yourself.

The Re-creation Process

Let's take the Great Pyramid of Cheops in Egypt as our example and examine this process in more detail. Just as any other tourist would, you take your photos, ride your camel, go shopping, and admire all the external beauty and wonder of this ancient monument. But there's much more, the "inner" sightseeing as well as the external. Touring this way, with "awareness," you will return home not just with photos and memories, but also with a more evolved self.

Say you go inside the Great Pyramid first thing in the morning, before the crowds, either on your own or with a small group. After a long steep walk up two shafts inside the Pyramid, finally you enter the King's Chamber. It's barren except for a plain looking granite sarcophagus, devoid of ornamentation. More than one tourist, looking only with eternal eyes, stares at the near empty chamber and exclaims "All this way just for this?" or "Is this it?"

You sense, however, the emptiness of this chamber is not all there is. You sense the etheric energy that pulsates through the chamber as you take the time to be quiet, and open your "awareness" to its non-physical dimensions. You start to hear and appreciate all that is said in the stillness of this wondrous place. The communication comes from within you, from your "Higher Divine Self," (or whatever you wish to call it) and simultaneously from within the structures and spaces of the Pyramid, engulfing the senses. The messages are not necessarily in words but rather come in impressions and feelings.

Transformation—Change in Self

The Great Pyramid was created, among other reasons, to affect or influence, all aspects of Self. Some levels of The Great Pyramid's special energy and consciousness can communicate to, and affect your physical body. This includes the organs and cells, even the atoms and molecules. You can feel it not only "down to your bones" as the old expression goes, but much deeper within and throughout your body. Also affected are all the parts of your personality—including your emotions, your senses, and your thoughts. Your brain may or may not be aware of all of this energy and consciousness-interaction and communication. Regardless, it takes place, and with it the alchemical process that can bring about transformation of the Self.

This inner communication and energy interaction simultaneously takes place with your "Higher Divine Self" (again, whatever you want to call it.) In this great transducer, the Great Pyramid, it's likely that you may experience this energy interaction, and the presence of your own "Higher Divine Self" more strongly than ever before.

One of the magical qualities of the King's Chamber of the Great Pyramids is that it magnifies to the mind and to your personality awareness of the union and communion of the Divine within you and the Divine of the Cosmos. As you learn to integrate with your "Higher Divine Self," you may even say to yourself by the time you walk out of the King's Chamber, "The Father, Mother and I are one."

Energy Interactions

The experiences and energy-interactions you have just undergone, whether you were aware of them or not, to a greater or lesser degree, become the building blocks for inner transformation and re-creation. This process, these building blocks, of course have many stages of its own. One of the first is that of "processing." The high quality energy you've been experiencing has a natural effect of setting in motion low density energy (states of consciousness) in you that are ready to go.

Worn patterns of your personality that bring about anger, fear, hate, etc. may be ready to be let go. They come to the surface on their way to being processed in this high-quality energy field. However, there must be a willingness to let them go! It may be that traumas come up temporarily as part of the "inner cleansing" phase of the process. They can be released without being the least bit traumatized. You may find yourself reveling in the ecstasy of high powered, high quality energy while you naturally and effortlessly discharge these destructive personality patterns. Or better yet, out with the old and in with the new!

Re-creation Results

Freed of debilitating energies and the accompanying states of consciousness, the most profound, and most fun part of the process now begins. The Re-creation of self. It happens spontaneously. You don't need limiting "affirmations" here. Rather, the proclamations of your "Higher Divine Self" begin to go to work for your transformation. You are jump started to the path of fulfilling your destiny—Re-creating your personality into something grander than your mind could ever imagine!

When you return to the hotel later in the day, or home when the trip is over, don't expect the glamour of showy outward signs of this transformational change. So what if you can't walk on water, or teleport home. Sensitive others will likely notice the changes with subtle signs such as the clarity or brightness of your eyes. Confirmation from others is not necessary. You will have the inner knowing of this transformation, a satisfaction that is immeasurable and far more valuable.

The transformative process may not all happen in the twinkling of an eye. So don't be surprised if you find it takes a number of days, or weeks, as the "processing" and assimilation of the "peak" experience at the "power place"® continues. But whatever you do, Do Not let denial of these inner "peak" events set in. You may have changed, and not even recognized it yourself. Frequently the "inner" shifting and process continues for six months or more after the initial, triggering events. As the "new you" evolves you will realize that it is actually nothing new. Rather, it is the "True You" that has been latent all along, now shining through more brightly into your everyday life.

The Re-creative process we've just been through in a general way can happen to anyone, anywhere, and anytime. A "power place®" like the Great Pyramid or Machu Picchu, while not essential, provides a trigger and then magnifies and intensifies such experiences.

Self-Re creation can happen anytime you take a holiday in its original sense, a Holy-Day, whether or not you are on vacation.

Written by Toby Weiss, Ph.D 1987

Acknowledgments

Writing this book was one thing. Publishing it has been something else altogether. It took twenty-one years of navigating the labyrinth of my internal world to anchor the courage to make public the experiences I have detailed here. Along the way were encounters with individuals who dropped a pebble into the book's energetic "ocean," sending out ripples that contributed to this publication becoming a reality.

I must begin with Neale Donald Walsch. Neale, your pioneering work in "Conversations with God" remains a landmark contribution to the landscape of self discernment and empowerment. Your very short yet potent communication to me in Crete during the "Life, Death & Beyond" conference in 1999 helped light the fires of creativity within me. I am deeply indebted to you that this book was even written! My profound heartfelt thanks.

To my sweet abuelita Grandma Rosie, your loving example provided peeks into worlds beyond the five senses, whetting my appetite for a life to be lived in full Technicolor.

To the team at "My Word Publishing," Richard Wolf and Victoria Wolf. My appreciation for supporting me in my first publishing experience, always getting back to me, answering all and every question, and for your confidence in me as an author.

To Inna Shirokova, thank you for your dedication and for your graphics during all these years of working together. I highly respect your ability to take a concept or vision I may have on a particular project and present it back to me with just what I had in mind. It was vitally important to convey the special energies of the "Shen" and the hieroglyph of the KA, and you did it!

To Emil Shaker, my cherished long-time dear friend, you have always had my deepest respect and gratitude. Acknowledged as one of the world's leading Egyptologists, in addition, you are the "Encyclopedia Britannica" of ancient Egypt's hidden mysteries. You and Toby meeting that spring day of 1984 inside Luxor Temple was truly auspicious. He experienced first-hand your extraordinary ability to make the temple "come alive." The love and deep brotherly friendship between you two over the years made for so many memories, laughs and good times while showing so many the wonders of ancient Egypt. Emil, even after 42 years of guiding, you bring an authenticity that irresistibly draws a person into the mysteries still present in these sacred temples. The love you have for these ancient temples, coupled with profound understanding of their hidden mysteries, provides a "key" to the person's own wisdom within. Throughout the years you and Toby spoke of writing a book together on ancient Egypt. It would be an honor to someday collaborate with you on such a book. My heartfelt appreciation for your constant support during this, at times, challenging re-writing process, providing your feedback and expertise in reviewing chapters that focused on aspects of ancient Egypt, and patiently answering my numerous questions regarding points of mythology, cosmology and hieroglyphs. Your thoughtful and expert input was invaluable, as was your perseverance with my multiple texts and emails needing to know the answers "right now!" I hold dear the love, support and understanding you've given me all these years.

To Gregg Braden, when I count my blessings, I always count you twice! Being the ground-breaking architect of the "Bridge" between science and spirituality, your empowering message of hope and expansive possibilities has helped propel multiple thousands around the world towards a deep healing beyond their fears and tears. When you and Toby first connected 20 years ago, you two instinctively "clicked" and thereafter had a mutual understanding and brotherly love. It is an honor to have you as such a dear friend. I treasure the ease of our heart to heart, mind to mind connection. Thank you for the support, love and caring that you have always given so freely.

To Herr Otto von Bressensdorf, where to begin to thank you. Healer, shaman, supportive and caring dear friend for over 13 years, a real planetary "healing force." Your potent intuitive wisdom and shamanic healing powers kept Toby and I balanced and in harmony with our life's energies and challenges over the years. You have literally saved my life twice now, importantly during the darkest of periods when I just wanted to join Toby. I especially thank you for your supportive love and healing energies and words of wisdom as I was deciding to take the big step to publish, and all the other times you're there for me. My deepest appreciation and everlasting gratitude.

To Harry Hover, beloved dear friend, where did 37 years go? When you and Ruthie met Toby for the first time in December 1982 to discuss Power Places®, who would have imagined the depth, width and cosmic connection we four would have? Harry, I am eternally grateful for your deep friendship, your love, your work at so many programs but especially your Peru, and our ongoing deep friendship and love, even after both our Beloveds have gone on.

To Walter Saenz, mi hermanito extraordinario. It was exactly 35 years ago that Toby & I met you in Lima while researching the Power Places® of Peru. We were looking for a tour manager to be our right hand person when we brought tours to Machu Picchu. We quickly surmised your top notch professionalism and expertise and knew we'd found what we were looking for. You're the "Papa" on site for our pilgrims, taking people by the hand and handling all logistics, freeing them to have wonderful lifetime experiences at the incredible ancient Incan sites including Machu Picchu. Even when times get intense, as happens when managing a group, your strength and clear thinking "parts the waters and rights the boat." I am very grateful for your continuing support of Toby's vision of a Power Places® experience, and the love you've shared with us as "familia" all these years, and greatly appreciate your continuing support, love and friendship.

To dear Jackie Cole, we shared a miracle that day on the Nile. I am so grateful that I could be there, in the right place, at the right time. There are at least 5 dozen people plus hundreds more that are grateful you decided to stick around! For many more years to come continue to spread the love that emanates so effortlessly from you. You will always hold a special place in my heart.

To Peggy Rose, your unwavering and constant support, and phenomenal professional expertise with all you do for Power Places® through the years has been of incalculable measure to me, as it was for Toby. My love, respect and deepest gratitude for "always having my back," and for the innumerable ways professionally and personally that you display the "high bar" you hold.

To Chris Giangrosso, I ran into you and when I said "It's Toby" without a word, just as I lost it, you enveloped me in a giant bear hug. That hug had such love and healing in it that in the moment I believed everything would be ok. You quietly said "I'm here for you." And you continue to be. I never forgot that hug. If people would just give an unconditional hug of love to others this world would be a much better place. Thanks for your heartfelt laughs and jokes which always bring a smile to my face.

To Chuck Brittain, I am so thankful that you shared your private journey of preparing to deliver your beloved cousin's euology. It gave me courage to prepare for Toby's service. What a friend!

To my family at Polly's at the Pier, my gratitude and love! Dear Sue, Yadinne, Shawn, Abby, Pam, Margi; your welcoming smiles, heartfelt "good mornings," nurturing delicious food, Sue-your traditional double macchiatos "beyond the Pale," impeccable service and taking such good care of me has comforted and sustained me. Not only during the rough seas when Toby passed but also through the many weeks immersed in the rewrites of this book. You all are truly awesome!

"Caterina" Kelly Stout—From the moment we met in Jerez, Spain during the flamenco class week, the light from your smile kept drawing me back. At some level, in your presence, a sort of healing would take place. Having had the same experience of losing one's Beloved around the same time has gifted us with a "simpatico" heart connection that is rare. I continue to be amazed at the light and the love we continue to draw out of each other. Your wise insights, pithy comments, stunning drawings and instant understanding of why I am reaching out is so deeply appreciated.

To Susie Dominguez, Franny Vilaubi, & Jeannette Ybarra, my dear primas, even though I am the oldest of us 32 cousins, you three are like my fairy godmothers. You were there to cheer me on when I was pushing the envelope with your traditional Mexican-American saint of an aunt "Norma" my mom. The first "family" teen-age rebel in the early hippy days. Your love and support throughout my life, especially meaningful when I shared about this book with what could be viewed as controversial content, has been healing.

To Mike, my dear brother, you are gifted with the "intuition" passed on from Grandma Rosie. Our deep mutual understanding of each other has been a blessing in my life. I will always be so grateful for your non-verbal and verbal love and support during the difficult journey of mourning and grief. Soon after Toby died you suddenly said one day, "You need to write a book." Little did you know I already had, this book!

To "Loretita,"dear sister, thank you for putting up with my shenanigans while growing up and for never once complaining that I never put anything away in the room we three sisters shared. I just made a mess, and you'd tidy up. How lucky was I! Your constant love, support and out-reach especially these last three years has been a steadying force, a rock for me.

To Mom and Dad, it would take a book to fully express all I am grateful for from you. For starters, it would have to be your unwavering support and unconditional love. And Mom, right up there would have to be your 5 star arroz con leche! You once said Mom that even though you never understood me, you just wanted me to be happy. In our last conversation before you passed away I told you that throughout my life "..you were the wind beneath my wings…" (from one of your favorite movies.) You replied to me that you had no idea, I in turn was shocked you had no idea! I am so thankful we had that last moment. Dad, your zest for life and search for adventures, even in the smallest minutia of daily life, showed me how to spot hidden treasures in the most unsuspecting places. You always wanted your Mija to just go for it. "Viva la Vida" (Live Life) was the theme you both lived and loved by. For this I am the most grateful.

To Rebecca, my Munchkin, you have taught me your own lessons about love. You were always your Dad's #1 Leo. What a lucky Gemini man he was to be surrounded by so much love. I am so proud of you, Rebecca. Love always, Mom.

To my beloved husband Toby, my soulmate, my hero, my best friend. After you read the first draft of this book over 20 years ago your words to me were magic. We were "two peas in a pod." I am in awe of the deep love and incredible life we shared. Indeed, we did "Viva la Vida."

NUT-Dendera Temple

There are Places
In this World
That have Proven
Their Power
To Energize,
To Heal,
To Transform
The Traveler.
They are Waiting
For you NOW…

Travel to PowerPlaces®

You are invited to travel with Theresa and a community of like-minded seekers to embrace the wonders of mystical ancient temples and sacred sites for meaningful "peak" lifetime experiences.

- **EGYPT** including The Great Pyramid & Sphinx, with deluxe Nile cruise. Accompanying and guiding the tour will be Emil Shaker, internationally renowned Egyptologist and the world's expert in the ancient Egyptian mysteries, their spiritual practices and cosmological views of life, death and the Afterlife.

- **MACHU PICCHU, PERU**

- **MAYAN PYRAMIDS AND TEMPLES**

- PALENQUE, plus PYRAMID OF THE MOON, PYRA-MID OF THE SUN

- Plus Tibet, the Amazon, Ireland, Japan, Crete/Greece

Email: travel@journeysoflifedeathandbeyond.com
Call: 1-800-234-TOUR (8687)

Workshops, lectures and seminars covering topics in "Deathwalker"

Theresa Dominguez-Weiss, and/or Emil Shaker, Egyptologist, are available for events, lectures, and workshops.

Contact: Media@theresadominguezweiss.com

Please state whether you are contacting, Theresa, or Emil Shaker, or both, the purpose of email, the name or theme of the proposed event, the location, and the proposed dates of your event.

Or Call: 1-800-234-8687 or 1-719-219-9818

Books of Interest

If you feel moved to delve deeper into some of the topics covered in "Deathwalker—Journeys of Life, Death and Beyond," you may find some of these titles helpful in seeking your own hidden wisdom within.

- Look for the long awaited book on ancient Egypt by Emil Shaker, Egyptologist (to be released 2021)

- "Man's Search for Meaning" by Viktor E. Frankl, MD, PhD

- "The Unconscious God" by Viktor E. Frankl, MD, PhD (English translation by Toby Weiss, PhD)

- "The Denial of Death" by Ernest Becker (Pulitzer Prize-winning book)

- "On Death and Dying" by Elisabeth Kübler-Ross, MD

- "On Life after Death" by Elisabeth Kübler-Ross, MD

- "Sleeping, Dreaming, and Dying" by His Holiness the Dalai Lama

- "Advice on Dying and Living Better" by His Holiness the Dalai Lama

- "The Art of Happiness" by His Holiness the Dalai Lama

- Freedom in Exile: The Autobiography" by His Holiness the Dalai Lama

- The Dalai Lama's Little Book of Inner Peace" by His Holiness the Dalai Lama

- "Proof of Heaven" by Eben Alexander, MD, (Harvard neurosurgeon)

- "Life after Life" by Raymond A. Moody, MD

- "Reincarnation and Karma" by Edgar Cayce

- "Many Lives, Many Masters" by Brian L. Weiss, MD

- "The Temple in Man-Sacred Architecture and the Perfect Man" by R. A. Schwaller de Lubicz

- "Going Forth Into Light" – The Egyptian Book of the Dead

- "The Dawn of Astronomy: A Study of the Temple-Worship

and Mythology of the Ancient Egyptians" by J. Norman Lockyer

- "Bardo Thödol—Liberation in the Intermediate State Through Hearing--Tibetan Book of the Dead

About the Author

Theresa Dominguez-Weiss, RN, FNP (retired)

Theresa Dominguez-Weiss' story begins in the early 50's, the first-born child to adoring parents in Southern California. Her mother and father were first generation Mexican Americans, whose own parents had fled to the U.S. to escape the Mexican Revolution. Growing up with seven siblings just south of Los Angeles, she was never short on adventure.

For 25 years she was involved in the medical field, starting at 16 as a candy striper, and then as a nursing aide as she put herself through college. She then achieved her dream of becoming a Registered Nurse and worked in emergency rooms, labor and deliver, cancer treatment units and many other areas of hospitals, always devoting herself entirely to her patients. On a quest for more knowledge, she eventually obtained an advanced certificate for Nurse Practitioner (FNP) from the University of California, Davis' Medical School.

Having extensively studied the field of neuro-immunology since the early 80's, she has also practiced various forms of subtle energy medicine and holistic medicine, in addition to instructing patients on behavioral and cognitive techniques to help with pain control, anxiety and stress. She believes that the practice of allopathic Western medicine in various medical disciplines, coupled with the over 40 years of in-depth metaphysical studies and energy medicine knowledge, allows a unique perspective in bridging science and spirituality.

Theresa left the field of medicine in the early 90s to help run Power Places®, an international custom tour company her husband Dr. Toby Weiss founded in the early 80's, after experiences she and Toby had at the ancient Mayan site of the grandmother goddess IXCHEL. Power Places® is now a commonly used term that relates to mystical sites around the world with special powerful energies, such as the Great Pyramid, Machu Picchu, Stonehenge, and the ancient temples in Tibet.

In "Deathwalker, Journeys of Life, Death & Beyond," she has woven together the tales of her extraordinary life transformative experiences, "peak" moments that have been springboards for a more meaningful life.

Please Leave a Review

Thank you for reading "Deathwalker, Journeys of Life, Death & Beyond," and I sincerely hope that you enjoyed it!

I would really appreciate it if you would please take a few moments to submit a review at Amazon.com.

If you did find my book intriguing, thought provoking, or just fun to read, please tell your friends or anyone else who might be interested.

I invite you to go to my website: theresadominguezweiss.com for more information on some of the topics included in the book, articles on "The World According to Theresa," my newsletter, and blog.

Hope to connect with you there!

In Peace and Love,

Theresa

Manufactured by Amazon.ca
Bolton, ON